....

THE GANDHIAN MOMENT

....

THE GANDHIAN MOMENT

RAMIN JAHANBEGLOO

With a Foreword by the Dalai Lama

Harvard University Press

CAMBRIDGE, MASSACHUSETTS

LONDON, ENGLAND

2013

To my daughter, Afarin

Copyright © 2013 by the President and
Fellows of Harvard College
Printed in the United States of America

Library of Congress Cataloging-in-Publication Data
Jahanbegloo, Ramin.
The Gandhian moment / Ramin Jahanbegloo.—First edition.
pages ; cm
Foreword by the Dalai Lama.
Includes bibliographical references and index.
ISBN 978-0-674-06595-6
1. Gandhi, Mahatma, 1869–1948—Political and social views.
2. Passive resistance. 3. Nonviolence. I. Title.
DS481.G3J255 2013
954.03′5092—dc23   2012004820

Contents

Foreword

Mahatma Gandhi has been a source of inspiration to me ever since I was a small boy growing up in Tibet. He was a great human being with a deep understanding of human nature. He made every effort to encourage the full development of the positive aspects of human potential and to reduce or restrain the negative. Therefore, I find it most encouraging to know that his life, in his deeds and words, continues to be a source of inspiration today in our rapidly changing world.

I have been deeply inspired by Mahatma Gandhi's adoption of *ahimsa*, or nonviolence, in India's freedom struggle. I have, therefore, put this into practice in my own efforts to restore the fundamental human rights and freedoms of the Tibetan people. I also admire the simplicity of Gandhi-ji's way of life. Although he was well versed in modern, Western knowledge, he remained an Indian and lived a simple life in accordance with ancient Indian philosophy. What is more, Gandhi-ji was aware of the problems of the common people.

I think of myself as a follower of Mahatma Gandhi. I consider the cultivation of nonviolence and compassion as part of my own daily practice, not because it is something holy or sacred, but because it is of practical benefit to me. Cultivating nonviolence and compassion gives me satisfaction; it gives me a peace that provides a ground for maintaining sincere, genuine relationships with other people. One of the most important things we all have to realize is that human happiness is interdependent. Our own successful or happy future is very much related to that of others. Therefore, helping others or having consideration for their rights and needs is actually not just a matter of responsibility, but involves our own happiness.

Another important aspect of the Mahatma's legacy is his insistence on the importance of truth. His practice of nonviolence depended wholly on the power of truth.

In exploring what he calls "the Gandhian moment" in politics, Ramin Jahanbegloo suggests here ways to turn hostility into friendship in contemporary politics and challenges the notion of there being no role for nonviolent action in Muslim public affairs. He examines how to preserve passion in politics, while deepening and enlarging responsibility for political affairs.

One of Gandhi-ji's key ideas is that the true subject of political affairs is the citizen and not the state. This is why the question of "duty" was of such importance to Gandhi-ji. On the basis of these ideas, Gandhi-ji succeeded in making the ancient Indian concept of *ahimsa* relevant in a contemporary civic and democratic context. An illustration of his success is the continuing pursuit of nonviolence in the human quest for positive change today.

In this book, the author examines how a greater democratization of global decision-making and introducing the concept of nonviolence to modern principles of sovereignty are intertwined and mutually reinforcing goals. His conclusion is that Gandhi-ji's ideas run counter to prevailing thinking among global policy-makers, who tend to rely on the use of force by showing how the practice of nonviolence is the sole reliable basis for achieving a stable peace in our world.

The Dalai Lama
2 October 2011

....

Preface

I began to think about the central themes of this book nearly two decades ago, prompted by two emerging political and philosophical trends. The first was the indisputable significance and diffusion of nonviolent dissent around the globe. The fall of the Berlin Wall and democratic changes in South Africa may have triggered naïve speculation about the "end of history," in Francis Fukuyama's famous phrase, but they also sparked constructive interest in nonviolence in international relations. The developments that followed drew attention to the relevance of Gandhi's philosophy of nonviolence and to whether the transition from unjust politics to more democratic politics could occur peacefully. The second was ongoing debate about the concept of sovereignty and in particular about differences between the modern concept of sovereignty—founded on Thomas Hobbes's and Carl Schmitt's ideas about absolute power, enmity, and the state of exception—and the idea of shared sovereignty as an alternative view of power. I began to address these changes in international politics by exploring how contemporary political leaders like Nelson Mandela and His Holiness the Dalai Lama could transform the Schmittian principle of enmity into amity. In this book, I consider the roots of such political work in the ideas and nonviolent experiences of Gandhi and Martin Luther King and also of some lesser known figures, such as the Indian Muslims Khan Abdul Ghaffar Khan and Maulana Azad, who directly challenged the conventional motto that "might is right." By including these latter, relatively unappreciated figures in this investigation of "the Gandhian moment," this book not only suggests a philosophical road map for turning enmity into amity in contemporary politics, but also challenges the prevalent myth of the absence and impossibility of nonviolent action in the Islamic public sphere.

To theorize about the Gandhian moment in politics is to advance understanding of one of the most puzzling challenges of modern statecraft: how to preserve the passion of politics while deepening and enlarging the responsibility for the political. Two questions motivate and guide this effort. First, what precisely is the Gandhian moment of politics through which an act of dissent and resistance to a sovereign becomes an idea of shared sovereignty? Second, what conditions and principles enable this Gandhian moment of politics to emerge and endure at the global level? These two questions structure the chapters that follow; I hope that what I write provides some answers.

··

CHAPTER ONE

Introduction

GANDHI'S INVERSION OF MODERN POLITICAL PERCEPTION

His physical body has left us and we shall never see him again or hear his gentle voice or run to him for counsel. But his imperishable memory and immortal message remain with us.

JAWAHARLAL NEHRU

Everyone knows the central ontological question: "Why is there being rather than nothing?" There is another, more obscure philosophical question, however, that the human race has similarly been unable to answer: "Why is there violence rather than nonviolence?" Why *is* there so much violence in the world today? Terrorism, religious and ethnic rivalries, environmental deterioration, economic crises, and unending international hostilities—all of which point to a world of global challenges and multiple threats. It is clear that in a world plagued by violence, we urgently need strong ethical thinking that insists on living up to fundamental principles in interactions among individuals and among nations and on changing the political realities that foster war. At a time when we are confronted by clashes of national interest, religious fundamentalism, and ethnic and racial prejudices, the principle of nonviolence may be our best bet in laying the groundwork of a new cosmopolitics. Though many continue to believe that nonviolence is ineffective against dictatorships and genocide, in the past several decades many democratic initiatives premised on what might be called "militant nonviolence," an affirmation of citizens' agency and a kind of neo-Gandhian quest for peace and justice, have achieved important successes. Perhaps never in the history of the human race has nonviolence been so crucial. Nonviolence has recently evolved from a simple tactic of resistance to a cosmopolitical aim based on international application of the principles of democracy. Given the global nature of the threats we face, the promotion of nonviolent solutions must be international. Achieving a global politics of nonviolence is the task not only of governments but also of civil society and intergovernmental, nongovernmental, and transnational organizations. Only a nonviolent society can work its way up to creating fully mature political institutions and realize lasting intercultural and interreligious harmony. At a time when terror conditions the life and mentality of at least two-thirds of humanity and violence influences our everyday culture, we cannot continue with the policy of the ostrich, having given up inquiring "whose responsibility is it?"

It would be a folly to expect nonviolence to become effective and durable, while the majority still thinks of politics in terms of the use of violence. It is true, as Hannah Arendt affirms: "Without a politically guaranteed public realm, freedom lacks the worldly space to make its appearance."[1] But it is also true that there is no long-term success in political freedom in the absence of morality. Thus, the political is dependent on the suprapolitical, which remains independent from politics. If politics does not remain dependent on the suprapolitical, it may end up in ruin.

That is to say, political events bring moral responsibilities, and in turn ethical views place their imprint on political decisions. Politics without ethics is pure exercise of power. It is only in combination with ethics that politics can be elevated as a public virtue. It is true that politicians eager to teach and impose moral behavior have committed terrible crimes. But spiritualizing politics, as Gandhi understood, is not about moralizing them, but is an effort to redefine them in terms of civic responsibility in an explicit public sphere. In his view, to engage in politics is to act in a civic role in a morally conscientious and socially responsible manner. Nonviolence is the key to this. The time has come for us to renew our commitment, politically, economically, and culturally to the Gandhian moment of politics.

In general, what I mean here by "the Gandhian moment" is the transformative power of nonviolent resistance in the hearts and minds of all those struggling for the opening of a democratic political space. Great public and political events, of course, might also be termed Gandhian moments. Think of the nonviolent changes inspired by mass demonstrations of people opposed to using military force in the United States, Eastern Europe, Latin America, South Africa, and the Philippines in the second half of the twentieth century. More recently, with the "Arab Spring" and the Green Movement in Iran, the world witnessed once again the mobilization of people, even with a mixed record of political success, seizing moral authority and relying not on violence but on courage and the truthfulness of their cause to confront tyranny. But in writing about a Gandhian moment, I do not wish to focus on such collective instances of nonviolent protest, but on the process of the mental and spiritual struggle that changes individuals within and helps create conditions in which the meaning of political action can be transformed. In this sense, the Gandhian moment is about reorientation, about individuals engaged in the struggle to reconceive themselves and their relationship with the state. To say that the Gandhian moment is at root about a new way of thinking might be to play into the hands of those who view Gandhi's approach to political and social transformations as naïve, unpractical, and utopian or to sound like one who romanticizes Gandhi and Gandhism, but rarely notices the muddy world of practical politics. But as we consider Gandhi's ideas and how they challenge the theoretical positions of the most dominant political views in the early twenty-first century, we should never forget that his ideas have had immense practical consequences around the globe. Nor should we make the mistake of thinking that Gandhi's ideas are only about strategy, about specific methods of avoiding violence. They are also relevant, for example, to the age-old divide between "private" and "public" that was theorized and sanctified by modern liberal thinkers like Benjamin Constant and blessed by American and French revolutionaries, which lives on in the ideas and practices of today's political parties. It is a dichotomy challenged by the Gandhian assertion that political action must take note of moral duty as much as individual rights. Gandhi opened up space for new kinds of political agency where politics is represented as a process of creative engagement with others to transform an unjust political situation into one that is more just. If, as is now clear, Gandhi sought to alter the meaning of political action by calling attention to the duties of citizens as much as their rights, this logically calls to mind the next question: just how did Gandhi determine the social and political role of the citizen beyond the state?

The core of Gandhi's theory of politics is to show that the true subject of the political is the citizen and not the state. In other words, in Gandhi's mind the citizen always stands higher than the state. This is why the question of "duty" remained of so much importance to Gandhi. In the Gandhian moment, the political subject embraces moral duty and frees himself or herself from ultimate obedience to existing political powers, thus inverting our common idea of who is sovereign. Gandhi famously wrote: "It is a fundamental principle of *satyagraha* [truth-force] that the tyrant, whom the *satyagrahi* seeks to resist, has power over his body and material possessions, but he

can have no power over the soul. The soul can remain uncon-
quered and unconquerable even when the body is imprisoned."[2]
Moving beyond fear allows the politics of Gandhi to move
beyond the sovereign law that creates authority. For Gandhi,
political subjects are not created by sovereign authorities, but
sovereign authorities are created by and share sovereignty with
politically active subjects. Gandhi described the precondition
for legality and legitimacy as the political consent of the citizens and not the power of the state, rule of the rule itself. The
problem for him is not just who rules, but the whole structure
of sovereign rule. Gandhi sought to detheologize and desecu-
larize the secularized theological concept of modern politics
manifested in the omnipotent sovereign that Thomas Hobbes
argued we must all obey or otherwise risk anarchy. Gandhi's
emphasis on citizens' ethical duties undercut Hobbesian political authority and required citizens under certain conditions to
disobey the state and its laws, undeterred by fear. Gandhi's
political practice was based on the taming of Hobbesian fear.
In *Hind Swaraj*, he wrote, "Passive resistance cannot proceed
a step without fearlessness. Those alone can follow the path
of passive resistance who are free from fear, whether as to
their possession, false honors, their relatives, the government,
bodily injury, death."[3] In order to give meaning to the concept
of nonviolence as a moment of "shared sovereignty" and to free
modern politics from the hold of godlike sovereign powers,
Gandhi presented the idea of shared sovereignty as a regula-
tory principle and, at the same time, a guarantee that there is a

limit to the abusive use of political power. It is also a principle that has meaning only with reference to the idea of responsibility. The major shift in focus that appears in Gandhian debate is from the common idea that political legitimacy is derived from political power to the idea that legitimacy is derived from the sphere of the ethical, an idea that gives crucial weight to the responsibility and duty of citizens to act ethically. Gandhi's challenge to the modern state was, therefore, not just to the ground of its *legitimacy* but to its basic *rationale* itself. The Gandhian principle of nonviolence is presented as a challenge to the violence that is always and necessarily implicated with the foundation of a sovereign order. Gandhi's critique of modern politics led him to a concept of the political, which finds its expression neither in the "secularization of politics" nor in the "politicization of religion," but in the question of an "ethics of togetherness" that brings together ethics, politics, and religion. This Gandhian moment of politics also leads to the possibility of a synthesis between the two concepts of individual autonomy and nonviolent action. Gandhi succeeded in making new words of ancient wisdom by turning the Hindu and Jain concept of "ahimsa" (avoidance of violence) into a civic temperament and a democratic commitment.

To understand all this better, to see how Gandhi viewed the advancement of democracy as intertwined with the goal of overturning our ideas about sovereignty, this book will proceed by studying various concepts at the heart of Gandhi's philosophy, show how he responded to contemporary critics and supporters, and move on to consider how some of his followers developed and used his ideas after his death. To that end, the next chapter contains an in-depth examination of principles of Gandhian politics, all of them linked to the philosophical core of Gandhi's nonviolence. In a way, nonviolence and autonomy converge in Gandhi's philosophy, for as the chapter demonstrates, Gandhi always saw the enemy as lack of autonomy, either individual or collective. Chapter 3 is a study of Gandhi's critique of modern civilization. As we will see, Gandhi developed the idea of "civilization" as a quest for the ultimate meaning of human existence and opposed this to the idea that modern civilization is simply newly acquired mastery over nature through modern science and over humans through modern politics. Gandhi also considered civilization as a dialogical process, one in which the East and West meet and transform each other. Chapter 4 moves from philosophy toward practice, tracing the development of Gandhi's public philosophy and the idea of "solidaristic empathy" as the unifying principle of his nonviolent democratic theory. Chapter 5 presents his ideas in dialogue with those of selected critics and supporters who were his contemporaries. Among his supporters, particular attention is paid to two Muslims unheralded in the West: Khan Abdul Ghaffar Khan and Maulana Azad. Chapter 6 elaborates on the legacy of Gandhian politics after his death and explores the Gandhian moment as a key to helping civic movements to form a politics of dissent and resistance while navigating the journey from enmity to friendship.

The conclusion touches on current affairs to discuss the rapidly changing world of violence in, especially, Iran and the Middle East.

The most important thesis of this book is simple: the Gandhian moment is possible. Nonviolence is premised on the existence of a universal ethical imperative that transcends religious and cultural particularities and is channeled through local, grassroots movements. The Gandhian moment was not particular to the Indian independence movement, the American civil rights movement, the dismantling of Apartheid in South Africa, or the plight of Tibet. It emerges, rather, as a viable and sustainable mode of challenging absolute sovereignty and domination in all times and places and for all peoples. To help root and advance these claims, the remainder of this chapter will take us back to the beginning of Gandhian thought, to Gandhi himself, partly to remind us of the connections between Gandhi's ideas and his life and times, but also to underline that Gandhi never thought of his ideas as relevant only to his own context.

"I am," affirmed Gandhi, "not built on academic writings. Action is my domain."[4] All through his life and struggles, Mahatma Gandhi expressed a profound respect for work in the public sphere. Some have attributed his love of public life to the fact that he was trained as a lawyer, but Gandhi himself put little stock in his legal training. In considering Gandhi's views on politics in general, it is necessary to understand that his interest in public work arose from his acute sensitivity to injustice and inequality and his passion for the ideas of freedom and pluralism. Gandhi's political work offers numerous lessons for us today. The overarching aim of this work was not to end the colonial domination of India, but to achieve something deeper and more spiritual: to bridge the gap between the practical and the ethical. Gandhi restored politics to its rightful place by emphasizing the harmonious interaction and compatibility among the political, economic, and spiritual. Whatever one may be tempted to believe about Gandhi as a political leader or religious character, it is clear that for him the goal of the struggle for freedom was not only to achieve political independence, but also to establish intercultural and interfaith dialogue among different religious traditions.

Gandhi did not practice law for his own financial comfort or pleasure. He similarly believed that the goal of the law was not to advance the narrow interests of a particular racial, ethnic, or social group, but rather the political and ethical education of citizens in general. It is no coincidence that alongside his struggle for political freedom from British colonial rule, Gandhi sought to fight for a just civil society. Gandhi developed a comprehensive view of political action that became the source of his strength. Although his personal trajectory prior to his departure for South Africa as a young lawyer in 1893 was one of gradual learning, what one can learn of this period by reading Gandhi's *Autobiography* is how early he began to question conventional frameworks in what he called his "experiment with truth." Gandhi recollected some of his early experiences with the prejudice or ignorance of his immediate entourage. Unlike many other children from a Hindu background, Gandhi had an Islamic childhood friend, a boy by the name of Sheikh Mehtab, who tried to convince him to eat meat to make him strong like the British. Also at an early age, Gandhi refused to consider untouchables as sinful, and he told his mother that it was wrong not to have any physical contact with them. These early forays into bridging cultural divides were isolated, but they had an impact on Gandhi's future struggles for Hindu-Muslim unity and against untouchability. Gandhi's sense of respect for others and his love of justice led him to study law in London at the age of nineteen and then on to South Africa. In South Africa, Gandhi increasingly distanced himself from the traditional methods of the Indian National Congress, which entailed petitioning the authorities and holding endless meetings, and instead developed his *satyagraha* strategy through his readings of Henry David Thoreau's *On Civil Disobedience*, Tolstoy's *The Kingdom of God Is within You*, and John Ruskin's *Unto This Last*. But the major lessons he learned arose from the humiliation and discrimination he experienced as a dark-skinned resident of South Africa. On the basis of his experiences, Gandhi came to the conclusion that unjust laws were to be violated because the sacred duty of every citizen was not to participate in evil. Thus Gandhi's conception of citizenship and his idea of a good civil society were inextricably linked to his ideas about justice. Gandhi knew only too well that injustice under law can be vastly more unethical than an injustice that is bound by no laws at all. All this helps to explain why between 1907 and 1913 Gandhi worked so hard to perfect a nonviolent technique for political action. Thanks to his nonviolent methods, Gandhi won himself a leading role and became an object of public attention in his relentless campaigns for the rights of Indians in South Africa. By the time of his return to India in 1915, Gandhi had become politically self-confident enough to take on the British rule of his native country and to try to put into place a constructive program for post-colonial India.

According to Rajmohan Gandhi, "Unlike other politicians, Gandhi had seen (from the start of his South African days) the interconnectedness, practical and moral, of three questions. Hindus would not *deserve* freedom from alien rule if they continued to treat a portion among them as untouchables; and caste Hindus were *unlikely to obtain* Swaraj [self-rule] if untouchables opposed it. And if they fought each other, Hindus and Muslims would neither *merit* nor *attain* independence."[5] Confident in his nonviolent methods, which he considered more effective in the long term than violent resistance, Gandhi thus seemed fully aware by 1915 of his ethical legitimacy and the practicality of entering India's political scene. Gandhi commenced his political life in India with a conception of politics as resting on a human capacity to organize a dialogical society. Gandhi's critical understanding of modernity and his intercultural approach to Indian traditions provided him with a strategy of connecting the elites and the masses through the method of *satyagraha*. Over the years, from his first campaigns in Champaran to help the peasants against British landlords to his later support for a strike over wages in Ahmedabad, and on until January 30, 1948, when he held his last prayer meeting before being shot three times by Nathuram Godse, Gandhi brought the ethical and the political into dialogue with each other. By breaking away from rigid caste distinctions and communal prejudices and by investing himself body and mind in the Indian public sphere, Gandhi thought and practiced a conception of active citizenship as a domain within which the public ceases to be a "private" affair and emerges as a potential forum where every member of the community can take part in the process of democracy. As Judith Brown correctly points out in the last paragraph of her book on Gandhi:

> Gandhi was no plaster saint. Nor did he find lasting and real solutions to many of the problems he encountered. Possibly he did not even see the implications of some of them. He was a man of his time and place, with a particular philosophical and religious background, facing a specific political and social situation. He was also deeply human, capable of heights and depths of sensation and vision, of great enlightenment and dire doubt, and the roots of his attitudes and actions were deep and tangled, as are most people's. He made good and bad choices. He hurt some, yet consoled

and sustained many. He was caught in compromises inevitable in public life. But fundamentally he was a man of vision and action, who asked many of the profoundest questions that face human kind as it struggles to live in community. It was this confrontation out of a real humanity which marks his true stature and which makes his struggles and glimpses of truth of enduring significance. As a man of his time who asked the deepest questions, even though he could not answer them, he became a man for all times and all places.[6]

Over his lifetime, Mohandas Karamchand Gandhi sought to become a world citizen. Out of his native Gujarat and later through experiments in England and South Africa, an original hero emerged into national and international visibility—a hero destined to lead his people and nation out of the bitter experience of colonial oppression into a new era of independence and freedom. Somehow Gandhi remains easier to manage merely as an Indian hero. It is simpler to explain his importance to future generations if we forget his broadest critiques of modern civilization and his search for the democratization of modernity that had already begun in 1909 with the publication of *Hind Swaraj*. Evoking the powerful originality of the Gandhian moment of politics necessitates self-questioning that is too easy to avoid. It requires acute attention to the vital and global manifestations of the democratic hope that Gandhi represented. His powerful determination to identify his life and his leadership with the cause of nonviolence everywhere, his call for the spiritualization of politics, his quest for the revolutionary transformation of religious and political institutions in India, and his attempts to unite the elites and the masses in India and to organize them into a visionary force for change—all these are the significant manifestations of the Gandhian moment of pluralist thinking and democracy making. Perhaps, then, the Gandhian moment needs to be broken free from all attempts to manage, market, and domesticate the memory of Mahatma Gandhi. We need to stop holding Gandhi captive to his common public image in order that he might help us to break free toward our most creative and dialogical future as intercultural communities.

Gandhi once said, "There is no hope for the aching world except through the narrow and straight path of nonviolence."[7] If we want to reap the harvest of dialogical coexistence in the future, we will have to sow seeds of nonviolence ourselves. More than half a century after Gandhi's death, we face a choice: either working to forge a peaceful human community in a plural world by speaking and acting toward the increase of human solidarity or preserving and enlarging the divide between communities and cultures by promoting or ignoring religious and cultural prejudices. Gandhi was led to believe that the future of civilization on this vulnerable globe was dependent on the ability of people of different cultures to live together in harmony, tolerance, and peace. Though he fired the spirit of nationalism and gave a clarion call to his countrymen to join him for the liberation of the motherland, Gandhi saw no conflict between being a patriot and serving humanity broadly. "Through the realization of the freedom of India," he said, "I hope to realize and carry on the mission of brotherhood of men."[8] As such, Gandhi's search for human solidarity and intercultural dialogue was an effort to narrow the gap between the logic of "we" and "they" while seeking, revealing, and displaying many voices in Indian society and around the world that expressed this common aspiration for solidarity and mutuality in all its facets: ethical, spiritual, social, economic, and political. Obviously, making sense of a plural world by cutting across various sorts of boundaries posed theoretical and practical challenges for Gandhi.

Gandhi's real challenge was to make politics and religion truthful by creating a dialogical bridge between the two. He believed that the process of fostering individual freedom and social harmony was only possible through the spiritualization of politics and the reintegration of politics within ethics. Gandhi described his conception of true citizenship as one of "the reign of self-imposed law of moral restraint."[9] In fact, it was not the morals of a sectarian religion that, according to Gandhi, were to be fused with politics, but what Gandhi called "the highest moral law." He referred to the two sides of his ethics as truth and nonviolence. Moreover, he described a moral action as "a matter of duty" and rejected any action "promoted by hope of happiness in the next world."[10] Not surprisingly, Gandhi frequently expressed his deep conviction that politics and religion were inextricably blended and that their separation resembled the separation of body and blood. Unlike those in India and around the world who believed that the quests for religious and social betterment could not unite, Gandhi refused to consider the spiritual and secular ideals as opposite poles. Mahatma Gandhi was different in that sense from most of the spiritual giants of India such as Sri Ramakrishna, Swami Vivekananda, and Sri Aurobindo. Gandhi treated non-violence as an absolute imperative, but this was not always the case with other spiritual leaders. Sri Aurobindo, for example, used passive resistance as a strategy in the struggle for independence, but he was not an ardent champion of the doctrine of nonviolence. Gandhi was nonetheless greatly inspired by the spiritualistic nationalism of some of these gurus. He stated that Vivekananda's influence increased his "love for his country a thousand fold." But Gandhi's religion was not confined, like that of so many others, to temples, churches, books, and rituals. It was closely related to the social and political realms. Gandhi was in this respect one of the few spiritual thinkers of his generation also to be a political leader. He once said that meditation and worship were not exclusive things to be kept locked up in a strongbox. They must be seen in our every act.[11] Surprisingly, what made Gandhi's thinking unusual in a secular age was his conviction that secular politics and spiritual ethics can be harmonious. He was bold enough to consider both paradigms of politics and religion outside their traditional conceptual frameworks.

It was the unique achievement of Gandhian thought to invert the Hobbesian approach to politics as universal desire for self-preservation. Gandhi essentially replaced the Hobbesian security paradigm of politics, which treats the state as a political agent responsible for implementing the requirements of human security, with his own paradigm of human solidarity. Accordingly, Gandhi's project of spiritualizing politics through nonviolent action had the twin objectives of bringing about a truly democratic transformation of the society and (thereby) securing an ethical social order. Politics, for Gandhi, was the search for the ethical. It was not enough simply to guarantee survival with the help of a protective sovereign. Gandhi's grammar of politics, therefore, was neither juridical nor technological; he adopted a new conception of society as a sphere of solidaristic relationships. He was quite aware of the fact that the search for human solidarity was not the same as seeking a social contract out of pragmatic self-interest. Gandhi, unlike Hobbes, did not view free society as a choice made by selfish people seeking to escape the war of all against all. For Gandhi, humans are not governed by their passions, but by self-restraint and self-suffering. "I have found," he wrote, "that mere appeal to reason does not answer where prejudices are age-long and based on supposed religious authority. Reason has to be strengthened by suffering."[12] Further, he distinguished between "self-suffering" and "violence" and developed the idea that self-suffering is proof of courage and truthfulness in nonviolent action. According to Gandhi, "Suffering is the law of human beings; war is the law of the jungle. But suffering is infinitely more powerful than the law of the jungle for converting the opponent and opening his ears, which are otherwise shut, to the voice of reason. . . . Suffering is the badge of the human race, not the sword."[13] This idea of "self-suffering" may be looked upon in Gandhian thought as an open recognition of the idea of interdependence and mutuality among social beings if one understands how Gandhi tried to explain what he meant by *sarvodaya* or "welfare of all." As for his politics, Gandhi's idea of service to fellow human beings is a negation of the utilitarian principle of the "greatest good for the greatest possible number," which leaves no obvious place for moral empathy and social self-sacrifice. Gandhi's emphasis on self-sacrifice and the capacity for service among human beings led him to a critique of modern civilization with its emphasis on the pursuit of power, wealth, and pleasure, as we will see in Chapter 3. A civilization as such, which termed itself as "modern," failed to take morality seriously as a guiding force. Gandhi described "true civilization" not as a linear progression of humankind toward greater prosperity, but rather as a manifestation of "good conduct" or a good way of life. In Gandhi's native Gujarati language, the word *sudharo* (civilization), as opposed to *kudharo* (barbarism), implies there is a higher mode of a conduct that guides us toward moral duty. The concept of *duty* is central as it connotes a responsibility that is to endure under all circumstances, and because it is duty that assists us in striving toward a better conduct toward each other. Gandhi saw a true civilization thus guided by duty as one that could attain the universal principles of morality. However, two questions remained for Gandhi: first, how does one go about emancipating modern civilization from the maladies it produces? And second, how does one build a new civilization based on ethics and morality? Gandhi's answers to these questions can be found in his major work *Hind Swaraj*, in which he attempted to reconcile the question of Indian nationalism with his theoretical vision of civilization. It was through his conceptual trinity of *satyagraha*, *swaraj*, and *swadeshi* that Gandhi sought to reconcile both practically and theoretically the ailment of modern civilization with a more sustainable and truer form of civilization.

The most famous of the trinity is *satyagraha*, or truth-force, which involves voluntary suffering in the process of resisting evil. As Joan Bondurant explains, "*Satyagraha* became something more than a method of resistance to particular legal norms; it became an instrument of struggle for positive objectives and for fundamental change."[14] No less foundational was *swaraj*, or self-rule. Gandhi believed in a political community that included self-institution and self-rule as basic elements that would lead to the growth of a truer moral civilization and a common understanding of mutuality. In Gandhi's mind, *swaraj* had to bring about a social transformation through small-scale, decentralized, self-organized, and self-directed participatory structures of governance. The third part of the trinity, *swadeshi*, or self-sufficiency, was considered by Gandhi as a way to improve economic conditions in India through the revival of domestic products and production techniques. As *swaraj* laid stress on self-governance through individuals and community building, *swadeshi* underlined the spirit of neighborliness. The three concepts were, for Gandhi, complementary. *Satyagraha*, for example, emphasized the principle that the whole purpose of the encounter with the unjust was not to come out the winner in a confrontation, but to win over the hearts and minds of the "enemy." Gandhi, therefore, believed that no true self-government consistent with *swaraj* could be achieved if there was no reform of the individual consistent with *satyagraha*. Similarly, on this premise, Gandhi argued that the modern state as an institution was enmeshed in violence. Gandhi's critique was not limited to the particular colonial state he was opposing, but was aimed at the fundamental rationale of the modern sovereign state itself. The key to this was, of course, the connection between political and moral sovereignty. Gandhi believed that the center of gravity of modern politics needed to be shifted back from the idea of material power and wealth to righteousness and truthfulness. In his critique of modernity, Gandhi saw modern civilization as promoting ideals of power and wealth that were based on individual self-centeredness and the loss of bonds of community that were contrary to moral and spiritual common good (*dharma*). Therefore, as in the Hindu concept of *purusharthas*, which refers to the objectives of human life,

Gandhi advocated a life of balance, achievement, and fulfill-
ment. Ultimately in Gandhi's political philosophy the two concepts of self-government and self-sufficiency are tied into his
political ideal of *Rama Rajya*, the sovereignty of people based on
pure moral authority. For Gandhi, therefore, politics remained
a constant process of self-realization, self-reflection, and self-
reform within the individual. It is a process of self-rule through
which citizens are able to contribute to the betterment of the
community. Thus it goes without saying that Gandhi's nonviolence presupposes a spiritual solidarity. Contrary to those who
claim that Gandhi was a reactionary, it should be noted that his
critique of modern civilization did not mean a return to the
past. It was actually a move forward in history and in human
moral progress. Clearly Gandhi not only saw the need for fundamental change in the modern world, but even recognized its
inevitability. It is one reason why his ideas have inspired people
around the world, among them Nelson Mandela, Martin Luther
King Jr., and His Holiness the Dalai Lama. King came to
realize that Gandhi was the first person in history to reinvent
the Christian ethic of love as "a potent instrument for social
and collective transformation." It was a short journey thereafter
to unreserved acceptance of the Gandhian technique of nonviolence as the only viable means to overcome the problems faced
by his people. King and Gandhi's life-practices challenge our
politics today. They both represent a different image of human
enlightenment, one that our world of violence direly needs as a
method of reform.

....

CHAPTER TWO

Principles of Gandhian Politics

That which is permanent and therefore necessary eludes the historian of events. Truth transcends history.

MAHATMA GANDHI

Gandhi is without a doubt the most original political thinker of the twentieth century. There are two aspects to this originality: one, Gandhi's originality can be appreciated when one recognizes his divergence from classical political theory; two, Gandhi appears as an original figure from the point of view of the vast political and philosophical traditions of India.

Gandhi's originality as a political thinker is best demonstrated by his deep concern with politics not as a struggle for power, but as a spiritual quest for truth. It is true that Gandhi was not primarily a theorist of politics but a practitioner of it. Yet Gandhi devoted his life not to pure action, but to the pursuit of ethical values and ideas such as self-realization and nonviolence. Gandhi's ethical commitments led him toward politics. His ethical convictions undergirded his political praxis and his continuous effort to reconstruct the social contract by the means of nonviolence. His relentless quest for truth made

him spiritualize the social and the political without dichoto-
mizing various fields of human interaction, specifically ethics,
religion, and politics. With ethical convictions that transcended particular theological or political doctrines, Gandhi
devoted his entire life to what he called "his experiments with
Truth" and to a spirituality of emancipation. As such, emanci-
pative spirituality became the main philosophical pillar of
Gandhi's conceptions of independence, nonviolence, and communal unity.

Satyagraha has generally been acclaimed as the first pillar
of the Gandhian political thought. But Gandhi never pre-
tended to be the innovator of this concept or that *satyagraha*
was a settled idea. "I have no set theory to go by,"[1] said Gandhi.
"I am myself daily growing in the knowledge of *satyagraha*. I
have no textbook to consult in time of need. . . . *Satyagraha* as
conceived by me is a science in the making."[2] Gandhi considered *satyagraha* as a technique of action for seeking truth. He
characterized it as a nonviolent struggle against lies and unjust
laws. According to Gandhi, the civic character of *satyagraha* is
maintained by refusal to cooperate with those who violate fundamental truths. As Raghavan Iyer says, correctly, "*satyagraha*
must resist injustice whenever and wherever it occurs."[3] This
resistance consists of fighting social evils and achieving a just
society in three ways: noncooperation, civil disobedience, and
a constructive program.

For Gandhi, the technique of noncooperation was based
on the assumption that no social, economic, and political injus-

tice can persist and endure without the cooperation of the victims, and that, therefore, the first step toward ending injustice would be immediate noncooperation. But for noncooperation to be effective, it should be based neither on ill-will nor on hatred: "noncooperation will become nonviolent only when it is resorted to for the good of the wrong-doer and will become effective if love is the motive that has prompted the withdrawal of cooperation."[4] Gandhi considered nonviolent noncooperation as a powerful weapon for struggle against unjust laws. For him, it was the duty of every *satyagrahi* not to cooperate with laws he considered to be immoral and inhuman, but he insisted that such noncooperation must not cause suffering to the adversary.

In the same way, civil disobedience, another of Gandhi's principles of *satyagraha*, was supposed to be "sincere, respectful, never defiant, based on some well-understood principle . . . [and] have no ill-will or hatred behind it."[5] Gandhi considered civil disobedience as a full exercise of citizenship. For him, it was a sacred duty of each citizen to disobey the tyranny that was repugnant to his or her conscience. At this level, Gandhi was very much inspired and influenced by Henry David Thoreau's maxim, which he often quoted: "That government is best which governs least." It would be wrong, however, to consider the Gandhian critique of the state as anarchist or libertarian. As David Hardiman notes: "While Western anarchists of Gandhi's day believed that a sharp revolutionary break was required before liberation could be achieved, Gandhi believed in gradual change through slow and patient constructive work."[6] One needs to add that Gandhi distinguished between individual and mass civil disobedience. According to him, "The chief distinction between mass civil resistance and individual civil resistance is that in the latter everyone is a complete independent unit and his fall does not affect the others; in mass civil resistance every resister is his own leader. Then again, in mass civil resistance there is a possibility of failure; in individual civil resistance failure is an impossibility. Finally, a state may cope with mass civil resistance; no state has yet been found able to cope with individual civil resistance."[7]

As we can see, Gandhi not only applied civil disobedience and noncooperation as strategies, but also treated them as constitutional rights that citizens could rely on against the abuse of power. In addition, civil disobedience and noncooperation constituted, in his mind, a means of moral improvement for individuals and nations, leading to genuine autonomy and self-governing institutions. Gandhi saw the way to self-governing citizenship as a passage from voluntary servitude toward acceptable laws and institutions and a form of political self-reliance. He regarded it as immoral to submit to unjust laws, even though the consequences for refusal to enslave oneself might include severe penalties. He wrote in *Hind Swaraj*: "If man will only realize that it is unmanly to obey laws that are unjust, no man's tyranny will enslave him. This is the key to self-rule or home rule."[8] But, according to Gandhi, reliance did not depend solely upon changing individuals and their good works, but also upon a program of institutional changes.

Gandhi developed a constructive program specifically designed to secure democracy from the very bottom upward. Gandhi was, in fact, referring to day-to-day social, economic, and cultural interventions, which he considered more basic than the political agenda in bringing about a truly democratic transformation of Indian society. He wrote: "I must confess that work of social reform or self-purification of this nature is a hundred times dearer to me than what is called purely political work."[9] It is clear that Gandhi aimed to achieve a completely independent India that followed his program for a just social and economic order. That is why he described the constructive program as *Poorna Swaraj*, or integral independence. This affirmation that *Poorna Swaraj* was foundational to democratic agenda sheds more light on the grassroots nature of autonomous civic movements in Gandhian social and political philosophy. Moreover, as Gandhi was committed to a participative democracy in a decentralized polity, he rejected the elitist view of democracy as merely the election of a minority by a majority. He knew from experience that all good governance is shared governance. *Satyagraha* was, therefore, a nonviolent technique of sharing power and self-governing. "Democracy is an impossible thing until power is shared by all," noted Gandhi. "Even a pariah, a laborer, who makes it possible for you to earn your living will have this share in self-government."[10] Obviously, Gandhi's democratic concerns went

27

far beyond matters of party politics and governmental policy-making. His approach to democracy was based on multilayered struggle and action to challenge all forms of abusive power. He viewed democracy as an ethical commitment that transcended narrow self-interests and enabled the community to improve its condition. The notion of exercising political power for personal gain was completely alien to him.

For Gandhi, the aim of democracy was to encourage and cultivate nonviolent action as a guiding principle for interaction among individuals and among individuals and communities and to foster the ethics of interdependence and responsibility. That is why Gandhi placed emphasis on the revolution of values rather than solely on the value of revolution. He believed correctly that national independence and political freedom should develop and sustain peace-building and facilitate a larger process of social and economic transformation. His fear of ethnic fanaticism and religious hatred went hand in hand with his concern for the spiritual transformation of Indians. He considered that an ethical revolution was necessary for India and Indians in order to rise above their self-interests and the problems inherent in relationships of power. According to Gandhi, nonviolence was about ethical self-realization and the search for truth. This search for truth was possible only through nonattachment to power. In this context, Gandhi affirmed the importance of ethical self-discipline, which he considered an essential precondition for self-realization and underlined it as a sign of moral strength. Moreover, he emphasized taking vows and considered them essential for character-building in politics and for social realization. For him, political life was a life of service and thus a life of humility. Gandhi argued that, "A humble person is not himself conscious of his humility."[11] Closely related to this idea of humility was his idea of "duty." Gandhi always emphasized the need to think of one's duties next to one's rights. "If we all discharge our duties," he asserted, "rights will not be far to seek. If, leaving duties unperformed, we run after rights, they will escape us like a will-o-the wisp. The more we pursue them, the further will they fly."[12] For Gandhi, therefore, in order to generate the power of nonviolence, one needs to find a harmony between rights and duties. "I venture to suggest that rights that do not flow directly from duty well performed are not worth having," he wrote in his journal, *Harijan*. "If you apply this simple and universal rule to employers and laborers, landlords and tenants, the princes and their subjects, or the Hindus and the Muslims, you will find that the happiest relations can be established in all walks of life without creating disturbance in and dislocation of life and business, which you see in India and in other parts of the world."[13]

Gandhi's concern with "duty" rather than simply "right" was closely related to his dialogical approach to the question of politics as a capability to organize society. As noted, politics for Gandhi was an ethical and spiritual task. Politics was supposed to be a means for improving socioeconomic conditions and removing inequalities and injustice and thus facilitating the ethical and spiritual development of individuals. In other words, Gandhi considered politics as the expression of an ethical duty by a person seeking his or her autonomy. As he construed politics, it maximized ethics and minimized relationships of power. Gandhi wrote: "To me political power is not an end but one of the means of enabling people to better their condition in every department of life."[14]

For Gandhi, village democracy (*Panchayat*) and self-government (*swarajic*) constituted the only alternatives to the soul-crushing power of conventional politics. Arguably, one could say that Gandhi suggested replacing the Western model of democracy with a uniquely Indian form where the village community provides the basic building blocks of social and political practice. Gandhi visualized a nonpyramidal structure of politics with the responsibility for governing placed in the hands of the people. His ideal of the *Panchayat* was formulated as "a complete republic, independent of its neighbors for its vital wants, and yet interdependent for many others." Thus, every village's first concern will be, according to Gandhi,

> to grow its food crops and cotton for its cloth. . . . As far as possible every activity will be conducted on the cooperative basis. Nonviolence with its technique of *satyagraha* and noncooperation will be the sanction of the village community. . . . The government of the village will be conducted by the *Panchayat* of five persons annually elected by the adult villagers, male and

female, possessing minimum prescribed qualifications. These will have all the authority and jurisdiction required. Since there will be no system of punishments in the accepted sense, this *Panchayat* will be the legislature, judiciary, and executive combined to operate for its year of office. . . . Here there is perfect democracy based upon individual freedom. The individual is the architect of his government. The law of nonviolence rules him and his government. He and his village are able to defy the might of a world.[15]

As we can see, Gandhi's vision of democratic order is sustained by the direct intervention of people in the public sphere. In other words, for him the guarantee of democracy is participation. Beginning with this alternative conception of politics, Gandhi also posited an altogether different theory of sovereignty. The organization of politics, as Gandhi elaborated it, can become possible only on the basis of a micro-sovereignty and the crucial participation of local communities. It is here that the Gandhian moment of nonviolence, not only as a form of civic resistance but also as a political invention, finds its full meaning. Gandhi asserted the inseparability of nonviolence as political resistance and nonviolence as a democratic construction. Similarly, he argued that nonviolence is the best means to invert democracy as an end, because "means and ends are convertible terms in any philosophy of life."[16] As such, the end of nonviolence, as with all other actions in Gandhian philosophy, is to prevent the community from becoming corrupted and tyrannical. That is to say, the exercise of nonviolent politics can be maintained, in Gandhi's view, only if it is combined with a powerful and just construction of participative democracy. Gandhi came to a unique realization that nonviolence provided the spiritual and the strategic means to bring about ethical change in the body of modern politics defined by vertical structures of power. Looking toward the India of his dreams, Gandhi turned away from modern politics by defining the goal of nonviolence in terms of the ethical, the self-realization of the individual, and the social.

Gandhi's quest for spiritual truth and moral self-realization thus went hand in hand with his struggle for independence and political freedom. Through his readings of ancient Vedic tradition, he translated the ethical concept of *swaraj*, meaning self-restraint and self-rule, into a category that was political and socio-economic in character. When pressed in 1931 to define the term more accurately, he defined it within its original philosophical meaning, while remaining attentive and truthful to its political sense: "The word *swaraj* is a sacred word, a Vedic word, meaning self-rule and self-restraint." In his daily application of this theological concept, Gandhi gave it an ethico-political character, which was already popularized by Annie Besant, the founder of the Theosophical Society. So wherever Gandhi spoke of *swaraj*, he understood it both in its ethical and political significance as self-determination, autonomy, and liberation. According to the Gandhian approach of *swaraj*, only he who self-realizes and transforms himself can be capable of liberating and transforming the world. This implies that, "the outward freedom . . . that we shall attain will only be in exact proportion to the inward freedom to which we may have grown at a given moment."[17] Political independence is, therefore, only one part of *swaraj*. More precisely, self-cultivation is at the heart of Gandhi's theory of *swaraj*. Here we see the extent to which, for Gandhi, the maturity of the individual and the development of the polity are interrelated. By equating self-realization with *swaraj*, Gandhi was conscious of the fact that building freedom and independence at a community level requires ruling one's self at a personal level. Going beyond the liberal meaning of individualism, as exclusively concerned with protecting strictly defined individual rights, Gandhi envisioned a polity where the link between the self-transformation of the individual and social reconstruction is evident. This persistent relation of the personal to the sociopolitical is a distinctive feature of Gandhi's political philosophy. As Gandhi asserted clearly, "political self-government, that is, self-government for a large number of men and women, is no better than individual self-government, and, therefore, it is to be attained by precisely the same means that are required for individual self-government or self-rule."[18] That is, for Gandhi, individual maturity attained by self-examination is the foundation of political maturity. This common connection between the individual and the community appears in Gandhi's idea of leadership as a kind of moral power that encourages examination of means and ends.

Gandhi thought the task of a leader was to educate the masses in the art of nonviolence. He stressed this point by demonstrating that "real *swaraj* will come not by the acquisition of authority by a few but by the acquisition of the capacity by all to resist authority when abused. In other words, *swaraj* is to be attained by educating the masses to a sense of their capacity to regulate and control authority."[19] One of Gandhi's primary concerns was thus to explain how an individual self as a moral agent in a political realm always stands in relation to other human beings. Gandhi realized that to be involved in politics was to be involved in a life that was also ethical and spiritual in character. And to be spiritual, Gandhi believed, did not require adherence to any one particular religion. His concern for spirituality in politics needs to be seen in the context of his view on religious pluralism.

Gandhi had pluralism in his bones and never made the mistake of rejecting or underestimating other traditions of thought in his approach to truth and in his stress on nonviolence. Although his thought had a strong Hindu core and contained elements that sat ill at ease with other cultures and religious traditions, he insisted that everybody had a right to interpret and revise his tradition of thought and that the spiritual quest of each individual went beyond a simple sense of belonging to a community. That is why Gandhi affirmed that, "There is in Hinduism room enough for Jesus as there is for Mohammed, Zoroaster, and Moses. For me, the different religions are beautiful flowers from the same garden, or they are branches of the same majestic tree."[20] That is what made Gandhi's approach unique. He was not always successful, but his dialogical engagement proceeded from a ruthless internal interrogation of his own tradition of thought. He was always free from the deadly vices of fundamentalism, dogmatism, and self-righteousness.

Gandhi rejected the idea that there was one privileged path to God. Similarly, he believed that all religious traditions were an unstable mixture of truth and error, and he encouraged inter-religious dialogue so that individuals could see their faith in the critical reflections of another. One of his notable innovations was the interfaith prayer meeting, where texts of different religions were read and sung to a mixed audience. If this provides evidence as to what sort of cultural pluralist Gandhi was, we can add that for him the sacred texts of all religions had contradictory trends and impulses, sanctioning one thing, but also its opposite. Gandhi confronted these different teachings by urging people to recover and reaffirm those trends that oppose violence and discrimination while promoting justice and nonviolence. For him, a culture or a religious tradition that denied individual freedom in the name of unity or purity was coercive and unacceptable. When some women were stoned to death in Afghanistan for allegedly committing adultery, Gandhi criticized it, saying that, "this particular form of penalty cannot be defended on the ground of its mere mention in the Koran," and he added, "every formula of every religion has in this age of reason to submit to the acid test of reason and universal justice if it is to ask for universal assent."[21] What Gandhi calls "the acid test of reason" is actually a form of experimentation with reason that, according to him, is a far better approach to cultural and religious traditions than empty reverence. Therefore, Gandhi was in favor of submitting all cultures to experiment to see how they are able to enter into dialogue with others.

This brings out another feature of Gandhi's understanding of cultural plurality. Aware as he was of the threat of individual self-centeredness and dogmatism, he also knew that there was a collective counterpart to this. It was rife in the colonial and imperial desire to civilize and to convert "others" and to disallow all forms of dissident voice. This explains why Gandhi broke with the tradition of "civilizational" discourse developed by his predecessors on the right and on the left. As Bikhu Parekh points out, correctly, "Unlike his predecessors, Gandhi's explanation and critique of colonial rule was essentially cultural . . . [because] unlike his predecessors, Gandhi insisted that the colonial encounter was not between Indian and European but ancient and modern civilizations."[22] Gandhi was willing to examine and endorse certain European values and borrow critically Western practices of dissent, but he was not convinced or frustrated by what many Indians considered the "superiority" of Western civilization. Since Indians were constantly challenged through colonial domination and the associated spread of Western culture, their self-esteem came to be tied up with debates about what was worth preserving in their civilization. Gandhi's cultural task, therefore, was as difficult as his political one. He had to show the practicality and relevance of Indian culture while being critical of its unjust, unwise, and impractical aspects. Furthermore, he had to help his countrymen to regain their violated self-esteem by renewing an indigenous system of knowledge and practicality, which had been marginalized and labeled unscientific and culturally backward by British colonialism. But he also had to devise alternative ways of seeing Indian culture and being Indian by privileging a culture of criticism.

Gandhi's writings about culture were neither self-congratulatory nor articulated false pretensions but were entirely open to self-criticism. He sought to create a public sphere in which the concept of "culture" was redefined and re-elaborated as a moral enterprise of individual and national regeneration. The spiritual component in this enterprise is obvious, but Gandhi was also a pragmatic politician who knew how to draw the line between the formal powers of government and the looser forces that operate among human beings. It is in the latter that he discovered the nonviolent strength of togetherness in pursuit of justice. He fully believed that "there are many powers lying hidden within us and we discover them by constant struggle."[23] He also sought to discuss ideas about the equality of cultures without being accused of cultural relativism. He was not a genuine relativist, but he understood that

37

the world was composed of different and interrelated cultures, each with something profound to give, and he tried to form a bridge among them based on common moral principles.

Gandhi believed in the toleration of other cultures in part because he believed that they are crucial aids to understanding and evaluating one's own. Gandhi always saw other cultures as equal conversational partners, and his plea to treat cultures equally arose from an intercultural spirit rooted in a creative interplay of concepts and values. His greatest ideas, such as *satyagraha*, were neither purely Eastern nor purely Western but came from a process of living between cultures. His ability to find a paradigmatic role as a path-maker and a facilitator of change in India reflected the cultural journey he had traveled. Gandhi was at the same time the "other Indian" and the "other Westerner." He was an outsider in both cultures and brought to his intercultural interactions his own sensibilities about where the cultural boundaries were and how "Indian" or "Western" cultural patterns ought to guide his behaviors. "I hate distinction between foreign and indigenous,"[24] wrote Gandhi. His achievement lay in embracing an "inclusivist" vision and a philosophy devoid of a polarizing "us" and "them." Certainly Gandhi was not without his sense of the "other," but he had too much respect for persons and cultures to render them into a dangerous "other." Central to Gandhi, after all, was the notion that the truth, power, and moral force of a movement are inseparable from the truth, power, and moral force of its actors. For this reason, Gandhi attached the utmost importance to heterogeneous components in the microcommunities.

Gandhi expected communities to be molded on the ability to see themselves in others and others in themselves. He considered such a policy essential to avoid the dangers of cultural conformity and instead move toward a genuine comity of cultures based on mutual exchanges and creative synthesis. According to Gandhi, this was a call for the simultaneous awareness of commonalities, the acceptance of difference, and the recognition of shared values. Tolerance of difference was vital to Gandhi's theory of nonviolence because tolerance for him meant, before anything else, an awareness of others, an attitude of open-mindedness, and an effort to know, understand, and learn from others. His understanding of religious plurality and cultural diversity went hand in hand with his cool reaction to a cultural conformity. As he once said, "I do not want my house to be walled in on sides and my windows to be stuffed. I want the cultures of all the lands to be blown about my house as freely as possible. But I refuse to be blown off my feet by any."[25] This statement of Mahatma Gandhi has particular relevance to our cultural situation in a globalized world. Gandhi's "house" can be understood as a metaphor for an independent and democratic self-organized system within a locally controlled, decentralized community of "houses," where communication between equally respected and equally valid cultures can take place.

The capacity to engage constructively with conflicting

values is an essential component of practical wisdom and empathetic pluralism in Gandhian nonviolence. When Gandhi identified *ahimsa* with love, as he did so often, he was actually underlining the concept of empathy as a dialogical response to the presence of the other. Empathy, contrary to sympathy or compassion, demands that an individual vicariously share in the thoughts and feelings of the other and temporarily become the other. Therefore, the first step of Gandhian empathy is to assume that not only are there differences among people, cultures, and political or social conditions, but also that people may have different value systems that need to be understood and respected critically. This is a practical application of Gandhi's concept of "religious pluralism." We find Gandhi's attempt to inject the idea of empathy into Indian communal debate as early as 1907 in an article in *Indian Opinion* in which he declared: "If the people of different religions grasp the real significance of their own religion, they will never hate the people of any religion other than their own."[26] The dialogical nature of Gandhian tolerance is expressed here in the idea of a "self-respecting" community that strives to remove its own imperfections instead of judging others. Therefore, for Gandhi, the acceptance of one's own imperfections was a call not only to cultivate humility, but also to foster pluralism. The reference here seems to be to the ethical content about which Gandhi believed there was substantial consensus in all cultural and religious traditions. Here, Gandhi's cultural pluralism is opposed to relativism, since it is based on a belief in a basic universal human nature beneath the widely diverse forms that human life and belief take across cultures. It also involves a belief in the fact that the understanding of moral views is possible among all people of all cultures because they all participate in the same quest for truth. This is why Gandhi affirmed, "Temples or mosques or churches. . . . I make no distinction between these different abodes of God. They are what faith has made them. They are an answer to man's craving somehow to reach the Unseen."[27]

Such a view is essential if we are to avoid the dangers of cultural conformity and move toward the recognition of shared values and the practice of cultural tolerance. If we agree that globalization is not just about an extension of market principles or an increase in capital flows, but also about the cross-border flow of ideas that affect cultural diversity, we can say that Gandhi's nonviolent approach to cultural plurality is a way to bridge differences and develop intercultural awareness and understanding in today's world. Of course, dialogue without listening and learning is merely a hollow discussion. Gandhian intercultural dialogue is an important step in being able not only to understand other cultures, but also to bring different cultures together and to find a common path toward the future.

Far from being a monolithic doctrine, the Gandhian perspective on nonviolence can be recognized as a dialogical and inclusive approach to the problem of politics. In the Gandhian notion of politics, there is a fundamental critique of the standard understanding of power. Gandhi believed that any strategy used to counter violence needs to begin not by meeting established powers on their own terms, but by embracing an alternative paradigm of nonviolence. And he sought here to distinguish between power, which could be legitimate, and domination, which could not. That is why he advocated a theory and practice of power based on love. In short, the Gandhian notion of power is informed by empathy and affinity: "The law of love, call it attraction, affinity, cohesion, if you like, governs the world. Life persists in the face of death. The universe continues in spite of destruction incessantly going on. Truth triumphs over untruth. Love conquers hate."[28] One can discern here a Gandhian distinction between two forms of power; namely, a physical power, which is a power to dominate and to exclude, and a spiritual power, which is a power to respect and to include, closely related to the quest for truth and nonviolence. It was through this new understanding of power that Gandhi established his language of politics and the preeminence of his nonviolence. In doing so, he also culti-vated a notion of an enlarged pluralism, where the voices and perspectives of everyone would be articulated, tested, and transformed.

For Gandhi, the propelling force of modern politics was neither the greed for wealth nor the quest for power, but for ethical living manifested in one's responsibility to the com-munity. It follows that for Gandhi ethical politics is an exten-sion of his spiritual view of social life. It is in this context that

Gandhi affirmed: "My politics and all other activities of mine are derived from my religion."[29] But he went on to say that: "The State would look after secular welfare, health, communications, foreign relations, currency, and so on, but not your or my religion. That is everybody's personal concern."[30] It is clear that for Gandhi secularism was not a narrow ideology, but an aspect of his enlarged pluralism and commitment to equality before the law. Understood in this sense, Gandhi's advocacy of a spiritual politics is to be seen in the context of a pluralistic community that integrates all different religious beliefs and minorities. It may be noted that Gandhi's understanding of an enlarged pluralism goes hand in hand with the inclusion of religious beliefs in the public space. It involves neither exclusion of nor indifference to religion nor a faith-based politics that would set up a monolithic code of conduct for all. So Gandhi would say: "Here religion does not mean sectarianism. . . . This religion transcends Hinduism, Islam, Christianity, etc. It does not supersede them. It harmonizes them and gives them reality."[31]

For Gandhi, religion is a continual search for truth, and different religions are different roads converging upon one truth. What is important is the spiritual journey toward truth and not necessarily the grasp of it. "There is nothing wrong," said Gandhi, "in every man following Truth according to his lights. Indeed, it is his duty to do so. Then, if there is a mistake on the part of anyone so following Truth, it will be automatically set right. . . . In such selfless search for Truth, nobody can lose his bearings for long. Directly he takes to the wrong path, he stumbles, and is thus directed to the right path."[32] In other words, Gandhi's spiritualization of politics is inscribed in his life-long nonviolent quest for truth. The relation between politics and spirituality, therefore, appears as not just an individual striving for ethical norms but also a struggle for the betterment of human community. Hence, Gandhi's insistence on nonviolent action as a cardinal principle of political praxis. A *satyagrahi* is one who holds firmly onto what she or he believes to be true by taming violence through self-suffering instead of inflicting violence upon others. As such, in Gandhi's eyes, a *satyagrahi* is one who is a seeker of truth and a person who believes in the force of discussion and dialogue. Gandhi's theory of *satyagraha* is embedded in a sense of caring for human suffering. Gandhi, however, unlike many political theorists, believed in the shared responsibility of the oppressors and the oppressed as a common burden of creating and sustaining evil. For Gandhi, no regime of untruth can last without the moral cooperation of its victims. A moral response to oppression would therefore be an effort of suffering love. Here were the ideals of the primacy of ethics in politics, the need to discern an empathic mode of action, and above all the essential principle of nonviolent compassion. But how did Gandhi expect this mode of nonviolent moral action to work in the political domain? What were the intended dynamics of his "empathic ethics"?

First, Gandhi's commitment to *satyagraha* as the only ethically valid mode of action for the pursuit of truth is only explicable in terms of his understanding of the balance and the consonance between the means of human action and its desired goal. This is to say that for Gandhi the well-accepted means-end dichotomy lying at the center of modern political theory is essentially problematic. The means chosen to struggle for a just society could not fall outside the framework of morality. For Gandhi, the so-called end of a moral action is already present in the very first steps taken to realize it. "Means and ends are convertible terms in my philosophy of life," wrote Gandhi in 1924.[33] Gandhi used this idea of convertibility between means and ends as the basis for his vision of a true *swaraj* rule. Gandhi knew that true *swaraj* could not be attained without moral growth and maturity. Moreover, if *swaraj* or self-rule was the end, political power could not be the ultimate aim. For Gandhi, a good polity was regulated through the work of small-scale communities, not by a modern centralized state monopolizing power. This was what Gandhi understood by the rule of *Dharma* (duty) or *Rama Rajya* (Kingdom of God). Writing in 1939, he described his ideal state in Thoreauvian terms as an "enlightened anarchy" with a minimum level of governmentality:

Political power, in my opinion, cannot be our ultimate aim. It is one of the means used by men for their

45

all-round advancement. The power to control national life through national representatives is called political power. Representatives will become unnecessary if the national life becomes so perfect as to be self-controlled. It will then be a state of enlightened anarchy in which each person will become his own ruler. He will conduct himself in such a way that his behavior will not hamper the well-being of his neighbors. In an ideal state there will be no political institution and therefore no political power. That is why Thoreau has said in his classic statement that the government is best which governs the least.[34]

This passage suggests that Gandhi gave little value to the liberal idea of representative democracy. In other words, the Gandhian concept of "common good" is formulated in the idea of self-realization and self-regulation of nonviolent citizenship. More precisely, the Gandhian idea of *swaraj* as a "common good" is not an Indian variant of the modern concept of citizenship tightly connected to the liberal-construct of a state of rights. Gandhi sought to understand citizenship as a form of political and moral agency outside the framework of the modern concept of the nation-state and in relation to an active exercise of dissent. Intriguingly, we witness with Gandhian politics an epistemological rupture with the unitary logic of modern sovereignty as a realm of national rights. Actually, the Gandhian language of "ethical citizenship" as a mode of being a nonviolent member of a community denotes an ontological effort to capture the idea of political agency beyond a national state. That being so, thinking through the practices of nonviolent citizenship goes hand in hand with reflecting critically on the problems of moral legitimacy in the modern liberal-constitutional state and how they manifest a clear failure to connect the ethical and the political. The Jallianwala Bagh or Amritsar massacre of April 13, 1919, which involved the killing of hundreds of unarmed, defenseless Indians by a senior military officer, convinced Gandhi of the unethical and inhospitable nature of the modern state. Gandhi came to the conclusion that the nature of the modern state was incompatible with man's moral nature. One can grasp here Gandhi's sense of "ethical citizenship" as a spiritualized and decentralized form of political agency. In contrasting his conception of citizen as a moral being who had the duty to support good, Gandhi devoted considerable attention to the formulation of a new social contract as a community of interdependent choices and overlapping duties.

Gandhi's idea that democracy fundamentally involves political agency beyond the state underscores his idea that we must form our political judgments as members of a community, rather than as individuals who stand alone. Therefore, it goes without saying that for Gandhi all individual actions in the public sphere incorporate moral and social responsibilities that transcend the relation of the individual to the state. This is to argue that the best way to understand the Gandhian theory of democracy would be to emphasize Gandhi's concept of "autonomy" as a way of incorporating the social in the individual without necessarily including the state. That is why distancing the individual from his or her political agency as a member of the community denies the understanding of the ethical individual that Gandhi maintains. This is one of the most significant differences between Gandhi's democratic thought, based on the concept of duty, and the liberal understanding of democracy as developed in terms of the guarantee of individual rights. Indeed, the liberal distinction between the "private" and the "public" does not apply to the Gandhian theory of democracy. Unlike in liberal theory, the individual acting as an autonomous agent in the Gandhian approach has a duty to the community that must inform all moral decisions and political actions. Hence, for Gandhi, democratic action finds its base not at the level of the state, but at the societal/ communal level as it is intertwined with the individual. This is most apparent in the way in which Gandhi transcends the line of separation between the communal and the individual. According to him, "Individuality is and is not even as each drop in the ocean is an individual and is not. It is not because apart from the ocean it has no existence. It is because the ocean has no existence, if the drop has not, i.e. has no individuality. They are beautifully interdependent."[35] Understanding Gandhi's ethical approach to the idea of democracy as praxis helps us to understand his solution to the dilemma of the division between the citizen and the state. Once again with Gandhi the emphasis is on the political community as the culmination of self-realization and self-rule rather than on the institution of the state as an instrument of fear or as a watchdog of individual liberties. The idea was not only, as he explained on countless occasions, that India had to create a national state, but to create a just civil society where rights and duties will not stand in opposition to each other.

In contrast with the Hobbesian or Rousseauist ideas of consent as fear or will, Gandhi defined a political community as a complex organization of mutuality and solidarity. As moral beings, each citizen has a duty to support the law as long as it is not unjust or morally unacceptable. According to Gandhi, "Most men do not understand the complicated machinery of the government. They do not realize that every citizen silently but nevertheless surely sustains the government of the day in ways of which he has no knowledge. Every citizen therefore renders himself responsible for every act of his government. And it is quite proper to support it so long as the actions of the government are bearable. But when they hurt him or his nation, it becomes his duty to withdraw his support."[36] Gandhi argued that all citizens are responsible for the immoral character of the state. Furthermore, he believed that an unjust law was an insult to the self-respect, dignity, and conscience of citizens, creating an unacceptable divide between the individual and his or her experiment with truth.

As we can see, Gandhi moved far beyond the accepted conceptions of statehood and citizenship by generating an idea of political relationships based on a shared moral commitment to truth. As he said: "Rulers, if they are bad, are so not necessarily or wholly by reason of birth, but largely because of their environment. But the environment are we—the people who make the rulers what they are. They are thus an exaggerated edition of what we are in the aggregate. If we will reform ourselves, the rulers will automatically do so."[37] *Swaraj*, or the true politics of empathy and solidarity, was only possible within an ethical polity in which citizens were ethically committed to self-regulate and self-legislate their political affairs while not betraying their self-respect and their duty of vigilance on the state. According to Gandhi, "Real *swaraj* will not come by the acquisition of authority by a few but by the acquisition of the capacity by all to resist authority when it is abused. In other words *swaraj* is to be attained by educating the masses to a sense of their capacity to regulate and control authority."[38] Within this framework of thought, a theoretical effort to identify a strategy for thinking through the meaning of politics beyond the legal boundaries of the modern national state reinforces the Gandhian characterization of ethical citizenship. Indeed, Gandhi acknowledged the fact that a political community should privilege a sense of reciprocity and mutuality as a nursery of civic virtues instead of endorsing the spirit of national sovereignty and state authority. Gandhi rejected a pyramidal form of community building and believed in the organization of collective affairs as an ensemble of self-governing and self-determining local communities: "In this structure composed of innumerable villages, there will be eye-widening, never-ascending circles. Life will not be a pyramid with the apex sustained by the bottom. But it will be an oceanic circle whose center will be the individuals.... Therefore, the outermost circumference will not wield power to crush the inner circle, but will give strength to all within and derive its own strength from it."[39] Gandhi insisted on a federally bounded community defined in terms of "expanding circles." The whole is, therefore, composed as a unity of unities constructed along the lines of a strong community enforced and sustained by a sense of justice. In this sense, the Archimedean point of Gandhian politics is a space of shared political judgment that is determined neither by historical necessity nor by normative rationality but by a moral claim to truthfulness and justice. This moral claim is, for Gandhi, a necessary reminder to reenergize the spirit of democracy, beyond what is possible in a state-centered liberal democracy, to improve a modern world suffering from a deficit of equality and justice. Gandhi thus opens up the possibility of reimagining the polity as a community of moral citizens with a sense of justice as empathy. Gandhi introduces here a culture of citizenship as one of dialogue and cooperation that makes sense of democratic agency as mutual recognition among members of a community who govern themselves by recognizing one another as moral persons.

Gandhi observed this empathic mutuality as a harmonious balance between respect for oneself and respect for others. It is this recognition of another as equally capable of self-realization and self-rule that gives rise to Gandhi's sense of community as the bedrock of ethical polity. Without this empathic role, the fundamental ethical capacity of policy-making would be entirely reduced to reciprocal egoism and an ensemble of self-interests. As we noted previously, this is where Gandhi found his constant frame of reference for his critique of modern civilization and its unethical character. It is important to recognize that for Gandhi there was a paradigmatic difference between modern civilization and what he considered to be the true meaning of civilization as a moral construct. According to Gandhi, the possibility of moral and spiritual life was the criterion of an ideal civilization. Persuaded that modern civilization had denuded life of its spiritual dimension, Gandhi was deeply puzzled by the violent nature of human relations in the modern world. As such, he embarked theoretically upon a critical analysis of modern civilization in its moral, spiritual, and political aspects in order to revive the ancient values of Indian civilization as eternal principles of a universal civilization.

CHAPTER THREE

The Critique of Modern Civilization

*The fatal metaphor of progress, which means leaving
things behind us, has utterly obscured the real idea of
growth, which means leaving things inside us.*

G. K. CHESTERTON

A study of Gandhi's critique of modern political thought would
be incomplete without an understanding of his critique of
modern civilization. According to Gandhi, modern civilization was responsible for a dangerous centralization and con-
centration of economic and political power. This went hand in
hand with a culture of self-interest, exemplified by the quest
for wealth and selfish pleasures and represented by the maxims
of "might is right" and "the survival of the fittest."[1] Gandhi
believed that widespread violence was the natural consequence
of these features of modern civilization. For Gandhi, the message was clear: the flourishing of humanity depended on
adopting a critique of violence and modern civilization and
mounting a defense of moral civilization. These two points are
set forth as the starting points of Gandhian philosophy in his
seminal work, *Hind Swaraj*. Gandhi wrote this one-hundred-

page book on his return voyage to South Africa in 1909, developing in it a particularly powerful and elegant expression of his worldview. His intentions in the book were multiple. He worked out his radical critique of modern civilization as a theoretical framework in which to situate his stand on Indian independence and his refusal to commit political violence. But it was also an effort to introduce Indians to their own civilizational values and to present an updated conception of *Dharma*. "My countrymen, therefore, believe," affirmed Gandhi in his preface to *Hind Swaraj*, "that they should adopt modern civilization and modern methods of violence to drive out the English. *Hind Swaraj* has been written in order to show that they are following a suicidal policy, and that, if they would but revert to their own glorious civilization, either the English would adopt the latter and become Indianized or find their occupation in India gone."[2]

Gandhi was anxious to teach the Indian nation that political violence was itself a greater threat to India than was British colonialism. He wanted to contribute to a reevaluation and redefinition of Indian cultural and spiritual values as principles to aid the reconciliation of Indians and Britons. In doing so, however, Gandhi defied both the principles of Hindu orthodoxy and the violent and unrealistic exigencies of Indian nationalists. *Hind Swaraj* can thus be read and interpreted at several levels. The first approach is what might be called a "strategic reading," highlighting Gandhi's response to Indian expatriates on the use of political violence. According to Anthony

Parel, these expatriates appeared to Gandhi "to be misguided Indians fully committed to 'modern civilization' who wished to fashion India on the model of Great Britain, Italy, or Japan."[3] In London on July 1, 1909, one of these expatriates, Madan Lal Dhingra, assassinated Sir William Curzon Wyllie, a former official in the imperial Indian government and a senior advisor to the British government on Indian affairs. Madan Lal Dhingra was under the influence of Vinayak Damodar Savarkar and his revolutionary ideals. Savarkar, an Indian anarchist living in London and a major theoretician of the revolutionary nationalist movement, sought to create a Hindu state directly opposed to Gandhi's vision of a religiously tolerant society where state and religion would remain separate. The assassination of Sir Curzon Wyllie shook London immediately before Gandhi arrived to discuss the South African Indian problem. While in London, Gandhi met with Savarkar. In fact, Gandhi had briefly stayed with a close associate of Savarkar's, Shyamji Krishnavarma, during his 1906 visit to London. Gandhi attempted to convert Savarkar to his vision of *swaraj*, but Savarkar rejected Gandhi's ideas and continued to promote Hindutva while Gandhi promoted nonviolence.

The second way of interpreting *Hind Swaraj* is through an "intellectual reading," one that brings out the intellectual roots of the Gandhian idea of *swaraj* and nonviolence as he develops them. Gandhi held great admiration for many Western thinkers; however, his thinking was not founded upon Western liberal philosophy, which emphasized the freedoms and rights of individuals, but on nonliberal thinkers and even more upon Indian philosophical traditions that were conceptually more holistic and communitarian as a whole. From the tradition of Indian thought, Gandhi derived the cognitive-evaluative principles of *satya* (truth) and *ahimsa* (nonviolence). Gandhian thought, as it is exposed in *Hind Swaraj*, has also wrongly been likened to utopian socialism and philosophical anarchism. It is true that Gandhi's thought is a philosophy of self-transformation, but if there is one thing Gandhi did not stand for, it was revolutionary violence. For Gandhi, any reform of society should correspond to a sincere attempt to live according to the principles of truth and nonviolence. Reformers should resist injustice, develop a spirit of service, selflessness, and sacrifice, emphasize responsibilities rather than rights, cultivate self-discipline and a simple lifestyle, and attempt to maintain truthful and nonviolent relations with others. According to Gandhi, the individual should subject each idea to the test of his or her own conscience and reason. The major Western influences on the Gandhian conception of *swaraj* and true civilization were derived not from the works of such modernist thinkers as Spencer, John Stuart Mill, or Adam Smith, but from the perennial wisdom of various nonmodernist thinkers. Edward Carpenter's *Civilization: Its Cause and Cure* and Leo Tolstoy's *The Kingdom of God Is within You*, which helped to shape Gandhi's views on the nonorganized character of religion and his commitment to nonviolent resistance, particularly influenced Gandhi's critique of modern civilization as well. Gandhi was also influenced by the writings of Henry David Thoreau and John Ruskin. In Thoreau's essay, *On the Duty of Civil Disobedience*, Gandhi found confirmation of his views on the violent and inhospitable features of the state and on the individual's obligation to return to his own conscience. Ruskin's *Unto This Last*, with its moralistic critique of liberal political economy, exerted a powerful influence on Gandhi's life, and he even translated it: *Sarvodaya*.

The third and last approach to *Hind Swaraj* is a "civilizational reading," one that connects Gandhi's civilizational analysis with his political philosophy and especially his ideas about pluralism. Gandhi raised his critique of modernity in *Hind Swaraj* against the backdrop of two interrelated questions: "How does political modernity cope with the plurality of civilizations?" and "How would the dominant framework of modern political philosophy have to be modified to accommodate the insights that might result from a multicivilizational perspective?" Gandhi sought to answer these questions by placing ethics at the core of his political and civilizational analysis. Sympathetic and critical commentators alike have suggested that Gandhi's *Hind Swaraj* is best understood as an ethical critique of modern civilization. Gandhi considered morality as an essential feature of a civilized society. He supported his argument by explaining that the Gujarati equivalent of the term civilization meant "moral conduct." According to Gandhi, "Civilization is that mode of conduct which points to man the path of duty."[4] For Gandhi, in other words, civilization and the peaceful existence of humanity heavily depended on the presence of ethics in diverse societies, which crucially entailed the curbing of violence. Humanity, he believed, had been evolving toward perfection by struggling against injustice and the unethical. But modern civilization had obstructed this process and cultivated a kind of violence in industrial societies, which had destroyed moral values and the ancient cultures of Europe. India, he thought, could yet avoid this fate and to do so it must resist the siren song of religious factionalism. As a strong response to the fanatic Hindus, he affirmed: "If the Hindus believe that India should be peopled only by Hindus, they are living in a dreamland. The Hindus, the Mahomedans, the Parsees, and the Christians who have made India their country are fellow countrymen, and they will have to live in unity if only for their own interest. In no part of the world are one nationality and one religion synonymous terms, nor has it ever been so in India."[5] Gandhi presented India as a land that had been and could be a model of intercultural civilization, a synthesis of different religious traditions that have managed to live together and influence one another for the better.

Gandhi feared the spread of violent modern culture beyond the West to other parts of the world, but also beyond human society to the natural world. Gandhi criticized modernity for its unscrupulous exploitation of natural resources and its lack of concern for nonhuman life. We have a duty, Gandhi believed, to show solidarity with and respect for the whole living world. For Gandhi, civilization, in the real sense of the term, consists not in the multiplication of wants that require unbridled economic growth, but in the deliberate and voluntary "restriction of wants." To be civilized is to exercise self-discipline and self-restraint, to put a brake on the pursuit of wealth and worldly pleasures. Modern civilization, in Gandhi's opinion, places the pursuit of self-interest at the center of our existence. It breeds unhealthy competition, exploitation, and alienation and too often requires violence to meet its goals. The pursuit of truth and ethics falls by the wayside. Gandhi's argument rests on a contrast between "modern civilization" on the one hand, and "true civilization" on the other. Modern civilization, according to Gandhi, makes "bodily welfare the object of life." In contrast, true civilization is and ought to be built on the basis of spirituality and morality, which in turn enables self-awareness and self-confidence and a cultivation of responsible and conscious choices in history.

Gandhi's rejection of modern civilization comes out most forcefully in his following statement in *Hind Swaraj:* "Let us first consider what state of things is described by the word 'civilization.' . . . Formerly, in Europe, people ploughed their lands mainly by manual labor. Now, one man can plough a vast tract by means of steam engines and can thus amass great wealth. This is called a sign of civilization. Formerly, only a few men wrote valuable books. Now, anybody writes and prints anything he likes and poisons people's minds. . . . This civilization takes note neither of morality nor of religion. . . . This civilization is irreligion. . . . This civilization is such that one has only to be patient and it will be self-destroyed. According to the teaching of Mahommed this would be considered a Satanic Civilization. Hinduism calls it the Black Age."[6] Gandhi correctly argues that the modern civilization is centered on the development of capitalism and industrialism as forms of exploitation of man and nature.

Gandhi's critique of modernity, technology, and Western civilization, however, did not extend to a complete repudiation of all their features. According to Bikhu Parekh, "Gandhi was . . . caught up in the paradoxical position of wanting to appropriate part of the 'spirit' of modern civilization while rejecting the very institutions and the social structure that embodied and nurture it."[7] Gandhi's critique of modern economic system was related to its inability to eliminate poverty while widening local and global disparities of wealth and despoiling the environment. The radical nature of Gandhi's critique of modern civilization has been interpreted by some as reactionary, manifesting a desire to turn back the clock. Gandhi, however, did not view his challenge to modern technological civilization as a rejection of the spirit of scientific inquiry. As he put it: "I have been a sympathetic student of the Western social order, and I have discovered that underlying the fever that fills the soul of the West, there is a restless search for Truth. I value that spirit. Let us study our Eastern institutions in that spirit of scientific inquiry."[8] It is interesting that Gandhi, who stubbornly refused with all his moral might a mechanized civilization, valued a scientific attitude while dealing with questions of social development. As leader of the Indian independence movement, Gandhi realized that independence required not just a shared identity and civilizational pride, but also a questioning, critical, and scientific spirit. Although he rejected scientism, Gandhi was firmly committed to the methods of rational inquiry and experimental testing. In his autobiography, he wrote specifically about conducting his experiments with truth with the utmost concern for accuracy characteristic of the scientific method. Gandhi's forceful critique of modernity, thus, does not imply a return to premodern modes of thought. He did not want a complete rupture with the modern mind and a wholesale return to tradition. Rather, his critique of post-enlightenment modernity is premised on the right to enter the philosophical framework of modernity through the doors of Indian history. The key to Gandhi's anti-modern modernism is that he sought to blend modern thought and Indian traditions. In doing so, he remained an outsider both to India and to modernity. His ideas are modern when compared with Savarkar's narrow-minded Hindu cultural nationalism and fundamentalism and traditionalist, with some contemporary political and sociological twists, in contrast with Nehru's instrumental modernism. Gandhi's vision for a thoroughly decolonized India entailed a kind of decentralized and de-technologized India with the decentralization of power and the encouragement of small-scale business, industry, and agriculture. Unlike Gandhi, who believed in village development, Nehru concentrated on large-scale industrialization and development. Nehru, well known for his conviction that rapid industrialization was essential to modernizing India, sought to achieve his goals through rational, scientific planning under the banner of five-year plans. An overwhelming belief in the superiority of a centralized approach to development marked Nehru's policy, which coincided with his belief that plans and programs had to be centrally carried out and communicated to Indians. Gandhi opposed such top-down modernization, but never in the spirit of Savarkar's Hindutva with its militant chauvinism and authoritarian fundamentalism. Unlike Savarkar, who identified "Indianness" and "Hinduness," Gandhi believed that all variants of fundamentalism, either Hindu or Muslim, reduced spiritual attitudes and civilizations to one or another version of dogmatism. Gandhi thought traditional fundamentalists were more concerned with power and with the mobilization of people for political purposes rather than with sharing people's aspirations and alleviating their suffering. Gandhi presented Hinduism as a pluralistic and all-inclusive idea. His vision of tradition pointed the way toward an India in which all the world's religions manifested complementary visions. The idea of a continuous and unified, but not unitary, Indian civilization drove his vision of India; one that Indians could draw on to loosen Western civilization's stranglehold. According to Gandhi, the materialistic values that the British Raj imposed on India had to be countered by the spirituality of ancient India. Time and time again throughout his writings Gandhi would invoke this theme of the need to revert to what he called India's "own glorious civilization," which he portrayed as far superior to anything offered by modern society. Gandhi evaluated India's contribution to human civilization in these terms: "I believe that the civilization India has evolved is not to be beaten in the world. Nothing can equal the seeds sown by our ancestors. . . . India, as so many writers have shown, has nothing to learn from anybody else, and this is as it should be."[9]

The strength of Gandhi's rhetoric here should not disguise how open he was, in fact, to elements of the modern West. In another context he wrote: "There is much we can profitably assimilate from the west. Wisdom is no monopoly of one continent or one race. My resistance to Western civilization is really a resistance to its indiscriminate and thoughtless imitation based on the assumption that Asiatics are fit to copy everything that comes from the West."[10] Nor should his belief in the strengths of Indian civilization be mistaken for complacency. His critique of the barbarities of the modern West has its counterpart in his various criticisms of Hindu society and untouchability. From the very beginning of his campaigns in South Africa, Gandhi regarded untouchability as a perversion of Hinduism. After his return to India and the establishment of his new Ashram in Ahmedabad in 1915, he banned any support for or observance of untouchability in his entourage. Later in 1921, he called on Hindus to "remove the sin of untouchability" in order for India to win its struggle for *swaraj*.[11] By the late 1930s, Gandhi was popularizing his Harijan movement in support of the Dalits all over India and supporting the idea of banning the practice of untouchability by law. Ironically, the Indian Constituent Assembly abolished untouchability on November 29, 1948, almost ten months to the day after Mohandas Gandhi was shot dead by Nathuram Godse, a Hindu extremist.

Although Gandhi was a born Hindu, and he described himself as a seeker of God as truth and later of truth as God, he was deeply interested in interreligious fellowship and advocated a proactive dialogue about various ideas and concepts in the domain of religion. He took true civilization to entail a federation of different religious creeds. For him, the compartmentalization and separation of religions was a poisonous consequence of colonial rule, doctrinaire attitudes, and modern civilization more broadly. Gandhi was a deep spiritual pluralist, and, along with his response to fanatic Hindus in *Hind Swaraj*, he went on to add: "India cannot cease to be one nation because people belonging to different religions live in it. . . . The Mahomedans also live in dreamland if they believe that there should be only Muslim India."[12] The resonances of more than one tradition and more than one culture can be heard in this statement, and it is clear that all religions were dear to Gandhi. In a speech at Buddha's birth anniversary, Gandhi proclaimed: "It is a very strange thing that almost all the professors of great religions of the world claim me as their own. The Jains mistake me for a Jain. Scores of Buddhist friends have taken me for a Buddhist. Hundreds of Christian friends consider that I am a Christian and. . . . Many of my Mussalman friends consider that, although I do not call myself a Mussalman, to all intents and purposes, I am one of them . . . still something within me tells me that, for all that deep veneration I show to these several religions, I am all the more a Hindu, none the less for it."[13] Reduced to its simplest expression, Gandhi's dialogical approach to the idea of religion and culture followed from his concept of truth. For Gandhi, there was a difference between absolute truth and relative truth, *paramarthasatya* and *samvrttisatya*. Gandhi considered absolute truth as an attribute of God and unknown to mankind. As such, glimpses of truth or existential experiences of it would be only particular instances of the absolute truth. Gandhi defined truth (*satya*) in the sense of being (*sat*) and pure consciousness. At first he said, "God is Truth" but later "Truth is God."[14] That is, truth is not just one of the attributes of God but "the" attribute or essence of God. Gandhi reminds us again and again in his writings that his entire life was an experiment with truth. Characteristically, Gandhi can be found in his autobiography interpreting the word truth not just as belief in God or adherence to a doctrine, but in its broadest sense, its meaning including self-realization or knowledge of self. The main thrust of Socrates's defense in court when he was sentenced to death in Athens for impiety and for corrupting the youth—"the unexamined life is not worth living"—runs across Gandhi's life and struggle as an ideal of ethical civilization.

Gandhi's conception of truth deeply conditioned his view

of human nature and the civilizing progress. In Gandhi's own words, to be civilized would be "to grow from truth to truth." In his view, it was not enough just to proclaim that one knows the truth. Civilization required entering a particular moral and spiritual state that is generated through adherence to truth. For Gandhi, civilization is truth in its dynamic form, unattended by violence. It is a philosophical principle that is ontologically prior to politics. Gandhi was well aware that many political and religious leaders thought differently and were far from convinced of the dangers of exclusivism and fundamentalism. Nationalists and religious revivalists strongly opposed meaningful intercultural dialogue. Yet Gandhi persisted, arguing that civilizations could be enriched by each other without losing their identity. For Gandhi, open and understanding dialogue had to precede, not follow, freedom and independence. A free India of true dialogical citizenship needed an existing foundation of communal harmony and diversity. To glimpse the harmonizing threads that bind humanity required confronting those civilizations and cultures that were blinded by deep-seated prejudice and hatred of the "other," and consistently pressing the case that the many shared concerns and values at work in each culture are all one for all mankind. Constant interaction among civilizations, Gandhi believed, could enable them to weave strands of diversity into the mosaic of a global civilization. Thus, Gandhi would have certainly have opposed a "clash of civilizations" argument that minimized human beings' capacity for dialogue and their potential to foster peaceful and tolerant mutual understanding among people belonging to different religions, belief systems, cultures, races, and civilizations. This was precisely Gandhi's understanding of the best of Indian civilization, and he had, indeed, grasped its fundamental strength and the secret of its survival as an innate capacity for creative dialogue, cultural pluralism, and diversity in unity.

These ideas remain disturbingly relevant. Fortunately for India and the world, Gandhi and his vision provide us with an ontological background against which to construct the meaning of dialogue among civilizations. Today when mankind is confronted with grim clashes of national self-interest, religious and secular fundamentalisms rooted in dogma and ignorance, ethnic and racial prejudices, Gandhian dialogue can reinforce the spiritual values of civilization and contribute to the evolution of ideas, to respect for diversity and pluralism, to the values of peace and democracy, and to a sense of human solidarity. Beyond India, Gandhi insisted on the idea of a global community, modeled as the joint family of cultures, as a response to the cascading crises that our world still experiences. One can make a reasonable claim that Gandhi's political journey was primarily a civilizational adventure with an ethical undertaking or, more accurately, a search under the umbrella of truth toward a new agenda of global transformation. Though the immediate civilizational task for Gandhi was to revive the dialogical culture of India, he also had a global vision of *swaraj*. He envisioned a world, not just a nation, of mutual respect and plural values. The universal character of a Gandhian polity was underwritten by his dual critique of religious fundamentalism and national particularism. But even as he thought globally, he kept individual self-transformation at the core of his politics. Gandhi's model of political emancipation was essentially moral. In such a society, the prime issue, then, is not just how the political is constructed, but on what ethical basis the political is founded. Suspicious of a celestial city on earth, Gandhi aimed at a social order, but also a future world in which "everyone is his own ruler"[15] and one that is made up of "ever-widening" communities. His ideal society of mutuality and tolerant reciprocity, which he named *Rama Rajya* (Kingdom of Rama), included a liberated, rather than simply liberal, polity that had attained a high level of spirituality, morality, and solidarity. It would be "an oceanic circle whose center will be the individual, always ready to perish for the village, the latter ready to perish for the circle of villages, till at last the whole becomes one life composed of individuals never aggressive in their arrogance, but ever humble sharing the majesty of the oceanic circle of which they are integral units."[16] For Gandhi, belonging to one's own community (*swarajya*) or country meant attaining self-determination, self-government, and ultimately freedom in a polity (*swaraj*). According to him, the maturity of a polity was, therefore, measured by the degree of moral self-realization of individuals.

This is not to say, of course, that Gandhi was indifferent to the mundane and material priorities of political work. Rather, he saw moral and spiritual revival and the harnessing of traditional Indian values as necessary aspects of improving people's material conditions. His experiences convinced him that the only way to create an ideal community of peace and prosperity was around the basic idea of *ahimsa* (nonviolence). Gandhi wrote in 1939: "A country whose culture is based on nonviolence will find it necessary to have every home as much self-contained as possible. Indian society was, at one time, unknowingly constituted on a nonviolent basis. The home life, that is, the village, was undisturbed by periodical visitations from barbarous hordes."[17] Gandhi had in mind a casteless egalitarian village community that he juxtaposed with India's caste-ridden society. He opposed the caste system on the basis of his support for what he thought of as the essence of the ancient *varnashrama-dharma* system. According to Gandhi, ancient Indian society consisted of a fourfold *Varna* order. "*Varnas*," wrote Gandhi, "are four to mark four universal occupations—imparting knowledge, defending the defenseless, carrying on agriculture and commerce, and performing services through physical labor."[18] For Gandhi, the system of four *Varnas* represented mutual support and service, and the *varnashrama* acted as a bulwark against westernization, as the kind of bridge between the moral and the political that we will turn to next.

....

CHAPTER FOUR

Gandhi's Public Philosophy

LINKING THE MORAL WITH THE POLITICAL

> *The test of friendship is assistance in adversity, and*
> *that too, unconditional assistance. Cooperation which*
> *needs consideration is a commercial contract and not*
> *friendship. Conditional cooperation is like adulterated*
> *cement which does not bind.*
>
> MAHATMA GANDHI

Gandhi was not a philosopher or a theoretician of politics in the strict sense of the term. His political ideas grew and developed as he struggled with the practical problems of power and authority that confronted him throughout his life. But his ideas were not simply ad hoc; they were rooted in stable ethical commitments and his steady belief that politics should not be separated from spiritual values. Politics without spirituality, according to Gandhi, would breed corruption, greed, competition, a mania for power, and the exploitation of the weak and poor. For Gandhi, political power was not an end in itself: "It is one if the means used by men for their all-round advancement." That is why "Representatives will become unnecessary if the national life becomes so perfect as to be self-controlled. It will then be a state of enlightened anarchy in which each person will become his own ruler. He will conduct himself in such a way that his behavior will not hamper the well being of his neighbors. In an ideal State there will be no political institution and therefore no political power."[1]

Gandhi's continuing study of Thoreau's *Civil Disobedience*, with its message that "That government is best which governs least," led him to the conclusion that political action ought to promote communally minded citizenship without diminishing individual autonomy. Gandhi insisted that an individual's autonomy is determined not just by minimal acts of political participation, such as voting, but also by a richer commitment to participation guided by such ideals as "service to the helpless." The Gandhian idea of service starts from the moral premise that individuals ought to renounce self-interest; Gandhi believed that there is no self-government without self-respect and self-sacrifice. Therefore, "He who holds his self-respect dear acts towards everyone in a spirit of friendship, for he values others' self-respect as much as he values his own. He sees himself in all and everyone else in himself, puts himself in line with others."[2] Similarly, Gandhi thought, the spirit of nonviolence leads people necessarily to cultivate civility and solidarity.

Gandhi reconceptualized political participation not only on the basis of new ideas about individual autonomy, but also on the idea that "the weakest should have the same opportunity as the strongest."[3] To achieve this goal, Gandhi wove together several requirements for the good polity. One is to decentralize power and render it accountable to the public. A second is to cultivate individual self-reliance, which for Gandhi required taking constructive acts against oppression. In his introduction to the booklet, *Constructive Program: Its Meaning and Place*, written in 1941, Gandhi described the Constructive Program as the construction of "complete independence by truthful and nonviolent means." The core elements of the program that Gandhi believed necessary included programs to create political campaigns and cooperative enterprises across communal lines, to liberate education, promote economic self-reliance, create a clean environment, and transcend caste distinctions, especially untouchability. The ultimate aim of the Constructive Program was to revive commitment to meaningful social solidarity and political deliberation in the hearts of the people. In other words, Gandhi's real politics of dissent was constructive rather than merely oppositional. He wanted to create a better India, not simply push out the British. What Gandhi came to call "pure *swaraj*" was formulated as early as in *Hind Swaraj or Indian Home Rule*, where he stressed governance not by a hierarchical government, but self-governance through individuals and community building. From Gandhi's viewpoint, adopting *swaraj* meant implementing a system whereby state machinery is virtually absent and real power directly resides in the hands of people. He wrote: "In such a state (where *swaraj* is achieved) everyone is his own ruler. He rules himself in such a manner that he is never a hindrance to his neighbor."[4] Therefore, "it is *swaraj* when we learn to rule ourselves."[5]

For Gandhi, *swaraj* entailed above all what he called a "disciplined rule from within,"[6] rigorous self-discipline, and a sense of responsibility. He believed that self-discipline was best instilled by daily participation in the kind of activities he included in his Constructive Program and by cultivating a fearless commitment to nonviolence. He wrote:

> Nonviolence is the law of the human race and is infinitely greater than and superior to brute force. In the last resort it does not avail to those who do not possess a living faith in the God of Love. Nonviolence affords the fullest protection to one's self-respect and sense of honor, but not always to possession of land or movable property, though its habitual practice does prove a better bulwark than the possession of armed men to defend them. Nonviolence, in the very nature of things, is of no assistance in the defense of ill-gotten gains and immoral acts. Individuals or nations who would practice nonviolence must be prepared to sacrifice (nations to the last man) their all except honor. It is, therefore, inconsistent with the possession of other people's countries, i.e., modern imperialism, which is frankly based on force for its defense. Nonviolence is a power which can be wielded equally by all-children, young men and women or grown-up people, provided they

73

have a living faith in the God of Love and have therefore equal love for all mankind. When nonviolence is
accepted as the law of life it must pervade the whole
being and not be applied to isolated acts. It is a profound error to suppose that while the law is good
enough for individuals it is not for masses of mankind.[7]

As we see here, Gandhi drew no clear line between individual self-improvement and national self-improvement, and
indeed his calls for one sound very much like his calls for
the other.

Gandhi's program for Indian regeneration involved a series
of interrelated strategies. Among these, the concept of *swadeshi*
appears as the most pertinent in the debate around the problem
of nationalism. Gandhi used the term *swadesh* to refer to the
idea of "sense of belonging" (*swa* meaning one's own, and *desh*
meaning the cultural environment in which one finds his or
her own cultural identity). According to Bikhu Parekh, *Desh* is
"both a cultural and ecological unit," and it does not "mean a
state or a polity."[8] In other words, Gandhi used the Hindu
concept of *swadeshi* as an alternative to the concept of nationalism. By doing so, he distinguished between "the spirit of
community" and "the doctrine of nationalism." So *swadeshi*
relates to things pertaining to one's own community and culture and not necessarily to the ideology of nationalism. Broadly,
it refers to the way an individual relates to the principles of a
civilization she or he shares with others. "Gandhi insisted that

since a man imbued with the *swadeshi* spirit loved his community and wanted it to flourish and realize its full potential, he could never be insensitive to its limitations; on the contrary, he was intensely alert to them lest they should cause its degeneration and decline."[9]

The Bengal Swadeshi Movement of 1903–1908 inspired the Gandhian Swadeshi. This movement began in the aftermath of the British decision to partition the eastern province of Bengal. The Swadeshi Movement not only inspired the Bengali political and literary elite, but it also gave an impetus to nationalist enthusiasm. The most famous and influential reference to the Swadeshi Movement in Bengal comes in Rabindranath Tagore's *Home and the World* in its female character Bimala's recollection of the event: "One day there came the new era of swadeshi in Bengal; but as to how it happened, we had no distinct vision. There was no gradual slope connecting the past with the present."[10] As with the Gandhian movement a few years later, the early Swadeshi Movement in Bengal promoted two ways of thinking and acting. One was to develop self-reliance with an emphasis on the constructive organization of village life. The other was to develop the strategy of passive resistance, which later became a creed with Gandhi and the Indian National Congress and was used more effectively in future confrontations with the British colonial administration. As inspirational as the Bengal movement was to Gandhi's nonviolent struggle, it is important to recall how early on Gandhi began to form his own conception of *swadeshi,* giving it shape particularly during his stay in South Africa after his readings of John Ruskin, Edward Carpenter, and G. K. Chesterton. Gandhi's early reflections on the concept of *swadeshi* were initially articulated in his famous pamphlet *Hind Swaraj,* where he made only brief references to hand-spinning and indigenous goods, but which interestingly set the tone for his later actions in India. Gandhi's early ideas made it possible for him later to reconceive *swadeshi* as such an important moral and political tool.

For Gandhi, *swadeshi* did not imply national selfishness and the exclusion of the "other." *Swadeshi* meant a self-ruled moral and cultural society that lives by the spirit of truth and nonviolence. Gandhi used the notion of *swaraj* to describe the social representation of *swadeshi.* He introduced a distinction here between *swaraj* (as autonomy, self-rule, and self-improvement) and nationalism. In Gandhi's mind, nationalism does not imply the quest for self-realization and self-improvement. Both nationalism and *swaraj* entail worldly involvements, but the latter is also a quest for truth and nonviolence. Therefore, beyond all forms of nationalism, Gandhi's approaches to *swaraj* as "home rule" and to *swadeshi* as "love of one's country" are spiritual commitments to the idea of civilization.

Gandhi's critique of modern civilization rests on the idea that it involves violence against oneself: "In Gandhi's view violence 'oozed from every pore' of modern society and had so much become a way of life that modern man could not cope with his relations with himself or other men without translating them into the military language of conflict, struggle, mastery, subjugation, domination, victory, and defeat."[11] Against the modern definition of civilization, Gandhi used his own definition of civilization as "a mode of conduct which points out to man the path of duty." Gandhi used the Gujarati word *sudharo*, which means "good conduct," and he opposed it to the notion of *kudharo*, or barbarism. Civilization, this all implied, can assist in the achievement of self-rule. More precisely, the rule of the nation by the nation is only possible when it is practiced in the framework of the idea of a true civilization. Gandhi saw a solution for Hindu-Muslim national hostilities within the context of what he called "a true civilization." Challenging Jinnah's conception of Islam as a criterion of nationhood, Gandhi argued that nationality had nothing to do with religion or language and was entirely a matter of culture, which Muslims shared in common with Hindus. Gandhi's affirmation of a common civilizational bond between Muslims and Hindus offers today a foundation upon which the new edifice of a universal thinking could be built. The genius of Gandhi's perception of the unifying power of civilization and solidaristic empathy helped him to see beyond divisions and boundaries of race, class, religion, and culture and to retain optimism even when violence between groups flared up. When he was asked in the wake of the religious conflict that accompanied independence if he was hopeful about the future of humanity, he responded by describing his faith in nonviolence: " 'Hope for the future' I have never lost and never will, because it is embedded in my undying faith in nonviolence. What has, however, clearly happened in my case is the discovery that in all probability there is a vital defect in my technique of the working of nonviolence . . . failure of my technique of nonviolence causes no less of faith in nonviolence itself. On the contrary, that faith is, if possible, strengthened by the discovery of a possible flaw in the technique."[12] In his self-critical reference to a "flaw in the technique," we can see Gandhi following his own teaching and seeking to summon up greater self-discipline and self-realization from himself as a moral agent responsible for putting nonviolence into practice.

However, nonviolence was for Gandhi more than a simple act executed by a nonviolent agent. He considered it as a spiritual weapon of self-purification and of empowerment. That is why, unlike violence, which is a mechanical and physical force, Gandhi described the force of nonviolence as mental and spiritual. The nonviolence he sought was not a static but a dynamic one, which endlessly continued to become more mature and unfold its myriad facets. For Gandhi, to practice nonviolence is to be responsible for the other, a responsibility that mere violence denies. Gandhi seemed to consider that it was in this call to responsibility in relation to the other that the possibility for genuine transcendence arose. But Gandhi also considered that nonviolence as an act of "holding on to the truth" entailed putting oneself in question. For him, the ethical subject must be capable of standing outside the self, fully open to correction from the other. For Gandhi, to embrace nonviolence is to renounce one's own hegemony and to achieve genuine transcendence. It was also, importantly, a step toward the restoration of justice, for Gandhi believed that the consciousness of every nonviolent self should coincide with the consciousness of justice.

In attempting to find a feasible concept of nonviolent justice, Gandhi followed the Hindu tradition of the *Bhagavad-Gita* and the Christian tradition of the *Sermon on the Mount*, proposing a redefinition of the ethic of *ahimsa* in the light of the unity of justice and mercy. The *Bhagavad-Gita*, a wartime counsel between Krishna and his warrior-disciple Arjuna, was Gandhi's favorite text. He looked into it for insights on the realization of the unity of self and other. The *Bhagavad-Gita* presented him with the idea of self-sacrifice, but also nonviolent resistance against violence. To Gandhi, Krishna of the *Bhagavad-Gita* represented self-realization or liberation through selfless action. As such the *Gita* became "an infallible guide of conduct"[13] to Gandhi and helped him to understand that politics (*artha*) could not be separated from social and personal morality (*dharma*). Therefore, his rendering of nonviolence (*ahimsa*) as justice and mercy stood in sharp contrast with the idea of justice as retribution. For Gandhi, the goal of justice was to seek a conversion of the soul of the evildoer without revenge. As he declared: "The purest way of seeking justice against murderers is not to seek it. . . . Their punishment cannot recall the dead to life. I would ask those whose hearts are lacerated to forgive them, not out of their weakness—for they are able every way to have them punished—but out of their immeasurable strength. Only the strong can forgive."[14] This leap from a definition of justice as a system of reward and punishment to a sustainable justice overflowing with mercy and compassion was a way for Gandhi to warn us against passivity in the face of political and social evils. As he said, "no man could be actively nonviolent and not rise against social injustice no matter where it occurred."[15]

Gandhi also drew on Christian values as he sought to guarantee human dignity against social evils. He first read the *Sermon on the Mount* while he was studying for the bar exams in London. He later wrote in his *Autobiography:* "The Sermon on the Mount went straight to my heart . . . the verses, 'But I say to you, resist not evil; but whosoever strikes you on the right cheek, turn to him the other also. And, if any man take away your coat, let him have your cloak as well,' delighted me beyond measure."[16] It would be closer to truth to say that what impressed Gandhi most was not Christianity or Christians, but Jesus and his teachings as seen in the Gospels. He found in Christ's message of love a deep affinity with his own belief in nonviolence. Gandhi, therefore, preached what Jesus taught against violent Christians, just as he used the teachings of the *Gita* against the violence used by fanatic Hindus. He emphasized the contradiction underlying the use of violent means in pursuit of spiritual goals. "Christianity is no Christianity," he stated, "in which a vast number of Christians believe in governments based on brute force and are denying Christ every day of their lives."[17] Gandhi's moral idealism aimed at living unconditionally Jesus's nonviolent means to attain justice and peace. But it also challenged him, as in the case of the *Gita*, to take seriously his responsibility for others and to work for peace and justice in a world so direly threatened with violence and devastation.

As a political actor with deep spiritual convictions, it was a priority for Gandhi to incorporate and if possible blend idealistic and realistic components in his thought and action. He was persuaded that the best way to solve the conflict between the moral illegitimacy of violence and the necessity of using it was to reform the individual and the society. In Gandhi's eyes the task should begin with self-reform and should end with the reform of the society. He saw *satyagraha* as a means of achieving *sarvodaya*. For this reason, Gandhi, who was an intensely spiritual man, abandoned the traditional Hindu path of contemplation (*sanyas*) and tried to bridge the gap between politics and spirituality. Significantly, Gandhi considered true politics a form of spiritual warfare (*dharma yudda*) in which there was no temptation for untruth. His real genius resided in applying the spiritual tradition of "experiencing the force of soul" to the political realm. Gandhi transferred the moral efficacy of voluntary suffering from mystical experiences in Hinduism and Christianity to the political arena. Understood this way, the essential and most original aspect of Gandhi's political teaching was to maintain that the key to his faith in nonviolence lay not in the practice of ascetic politics, but in his pragmatic experience of the political among other human beings. The combination of courage and sacrifice had a substantial experimental basis in the Gandhian struggle for nonviolence. According to Gandhi, the best way to convince the opponent of one's sincerity is to make sacrifices for one's cause. It is a strategy, he believed, that gains further power from the force of "dialogical empathy."

The Gandhian approach to "dialogical empathy" is two-sided. One side is the classical meaning of empathy: perceiving another person's experience of life through that person's eyes and appreciating that person's emotions under conditions of conflict. Dialogical empathy calls for understanding what is going on in the minds of your opponents and recognizing their human side, including their fears and insecurities. It is the very opposite of demonizing one's enemy. On the other side of the coin, dialogical empathy means trying to look at one's behavior through the other's eyes, recognizing critically one's moments of distrust, fear, and anger. D. G. Tendulkar reported on Gandhi's cultivation of dialogical empathy with a person who wanted to kill him in the following passage of his book: "God only knew how he would have behaved in front of a bomb aimed at him and exploding. Therefore, he deserved no praise. He would deserve a certificate only if he fell as a result of such an explosion, and yet retained a smile on his face and no malice against the doer. What he wanted to convey was that no one should look down upon the misguided young man who had thrown the bomb. . . . After all, had not the *Gita* said that whenever there was an evil-minded person damaging religion, God sent someone to put an end to his life? That celebrated verse had a special meaning. The youth should realize that those who differed from him were not necessarily evil. The evil had no life apart from the toleration of good people."[18] Gandhi knew clearly that nonviolent action is directed at eliminating evil, not destroying an evil-doer. Gandhi's own encounters with evil repeatedly showed that his basic philosophy of nonviolence was to love humanity and to not oppose evil with violence. According to Gandhi, nonviolence did not mean docile submission to the will of evil, but setting the force of the soul against the will of evil. He took this to be part of the self's process toward maturity. In the Gandhian praxis of politics, the self-realization of the mature self requires the maturity of others. The recognition of interdependence that comes with maturity makes nonviolent action the appropriate way of transcending the very process of antagonism. To put it more directly, Gandhian nonviolence is based on an ethics of reciprocity with the aim of dissolving antagonistic conflict. As such, it is not founded on a philosophy of "us versus them." On the contrary, it is a faith based on extreme moral courage that draws its strength from innate human truth and honesty. It avoids the adversarial, antagonistic, and often angry approach that leads so many people either to fight or to burn out. Instead, it attempts to uplift and energize people. The interdependence of mature people and their reliance on nonviolent action allows them to transcend antagonism and elevate their interactions to an agonistic space where they do not seek victory, but display deep respect and concern for the other without hiding their differences. The Gandhian strategy of nonviolence, therefore, presupposes a radical distinction between antagonism and antagonists. According to Gandhi, "The essence of nonviolent technique is that it seeks to liquidate antagonisms but not the antagonists themselves."[19] The long road toward nonviolence cannot be followed if one does not understand that the supreme goal of active nonviolence is to stimulate dialogical empathy and encourage constructive interpersonal contact between members of hostile groups. In this and other respects, it is clear that Gandhi practiced a form of "epistemic humility," a refusal to believe that he alone knew what was right and true, in his practice of nonviolent conflict management. Much of Gandhi's social and political activities were based on the development of this epistemic humility as an art of compromise. "All human life," explained Gandhi, "is a series of compromises, and it is not always easy to achieve in practice what one has found to be true in theory."[20] Gandhian nonviolence is thus a search for balance between epistemic humility and the need for action out in the open. Gandhi was very conscious in applying this epistemic humility against all forms of political and religious arrogance, while he ran it through his nonviolent management of antagonistic conflicts. Dialogical empathy, it should be noted, has two components: first, empathizing with the other—that is, appreciating the other's perception of the issues involved in the conflict—and, second, comprehending the other's perception of one's own role in the conflict. It is actually a move forward to the question of responsibility. In fact, a degree of responsibility, as a moral experience, is involved in this process of dialogical empathy, no matter how individuals transform themselves as they move from a passive political role to active nonviolent engagement. Responsibility, for Gandhi, precedes freedom because it leads us toward a just treatment of the other, the ideal presented by freedom should in turn reinform one's neighborliness toward the individual other. Thus, in the Gandhian nonviolent face-to-face with the other, moral responsibility for the neighbor has priority over any other social practice. Moreover, the process of facilitating contact between opponents and overcoming evil requires an appreciation of each other's self-experience and experience of the other. Following this line of thought, active nonviolence, in Gandhi's eyes, goes far beyond conventional or rote practices in a political democracy.

For Gandhi, living democratically was not merely a matter of living in a liberal regime with a representative government. It meant an active politics of moral commitment. This formulation can be clarified by something Nehru once said about Gandhi's view of democracy: "Gandhi-ji's conception of democracy has nothing to do with numbers or majority or representation in the ordinary sense. It is based on service and sacrifice, and it uses moral pressure."[21] According to Gandhi, a true government of service and sacrifice would be a stateless entity that would prepare all individuals to self-regulate. So he suggested a political structure that was not election-oriented and party-centered, but that would be regulated from within. This meant that he emphasized the participation of small social units in the political process. Furthermore, he insisted on welfare for all in contrast with the utilitarian emphasis on the greatest good for the greatest number and argued for creative cooperation and interaction to transform social and political structures. As early as in 1926, Gandhi distinguished his theory of *sarvodaya*, inspired by his reading of Ruskin's *Unto This Last*, from utilitarianism: "A votary of *ahimsa* cannot subscribe to the utilitarian formula. He will strive for the greatest good of all and die in the attempt to realize the ideal. He will, therefore, be willing to die so that the others may live. He will serve himself with the rest by himself dying. The greatest good of all inevitably includes the good of the greatest number, and therefore he and the utilitarian will converge in many points in their career, but there does come a time when they must part company and even work in opposite directions. The utilitarian to be logical will never sacrifice himself. The absolutist will even sacrifice himself."[22] In this regard, Gandhi held very clearly that nonviolence was not only about moral resistance against evil institutions, but also a duty to build up democracy from the base. Gandhi's approach to this question gradually became more pragmatic and more radical. Seen from the Gandhian perspective, democracy was a perpetual political, social, economic, and cultural pursuit, not the one-time construction of certain institutions that could then be left to run more or less alone. This form of democracy could not be realized and consolidated unless the balance of the ends and means was maintained. As a result, Gandhi was for a decentralized economy with an emphasis on "production by masses" rather than "mass production" and on a theory of trusteeship when it came to property. Gandhi conceived of trusteeship as a system wherein the individual considers part of his wealth in excess of his needs as being held in trust for the larger good of society and acts accordingly.[23] This flowed from his belief in the oneness of mankind but also from his conviction that economic policy and social behavior should not ignore moral values. He believed that, "Those who own money now are asked to behave like trustees holding their riches on behalf of the poor. The question how many can be real trustees according to this definition is beside the point. If the theory is true, it is immaterial whether many live up to it or only one man lives up to it. . . . Absolute trusteeship is an abstraction like Euclid's definition of a point. But if we strive for it, we shall be able to go further in realizing a state of equality on earth than by any other method."[24] Gandhi disapproved of the capitalist system, but he distinguished between capitalism and business talent. He affirmed: "We must not underrate the business talent and know-how which the owing class has acquired through generations of experience and specialization,"[25] but he also added, "Economic equality is the master key to nonviolent transformationary independence. Working for economic equality means abolishing the eternal conflict between capital

87

and labor. It means leveling down of the few rich in whose hands is concentrated the bulk of the nation's wealth, on the one hand, and the leveling up of the semistarved naked millions, on the other. A nonviolent system of government is clearly an impossibility so long as the wide gulf between the rich and the hungry millions persists."[26] As we can see, Gandhi's nonviolence was closely related to his insistence that we provide immediate assistance to those in greatest need. This is what he described as his Constructive Program, which meant building a new society in the shell of the old. Gandhi believed that the core elements of the Constructive Program could provide a series of transformative programs that embodied equality and the values of education and environmental sustainability for economic self-reliance. He took equality to include gender equality and transcending caste distinctions, especially untouchability. Equality also meant pursuing India's ability to articulate an overarching vision for cultural change, which would restore relationships among Muslims and Hindus and the Hindu castes. It was thus that, for Gandhi, *Khadi* (homespun cotton cloth) and *charkha* (spinning wheel) came to represent economic independence through meaningful local work, solidarity with the poor, and "simple living so that all might simply live." Gandhi furthermore described the message of *charkha* as "much wider than its circumference. Its message is one of simplicity, service of humanity, living so as not to hurt others, creating an indissoluble bond between the rich and the poor, capital and labor, the prince and the peasant."[27] It was obvious to Gandhi that with the Constructive Program, an "economy of love" should replace an "economy of greed." This certainly meant decentralization of the production and distribution of the necessaries of life. But it also meant putting stress on the idea of a harmonious society where diversity and cooperation are emphasized. Gandhi's ideal of a village republic implied participatory management and the use of appropriate, environmentally friendly technology. The New Education was also an essential component of Gandhi's famous Constructive Program, which presented his positive moral and spiritual vision for a new democratic society.

Gandhi's theory of basic education is an expression of his philosophical and political world-views and one of the key pillars of his ideal society. His ideal educational system combined his three concepts of *swaraj* (self-rule), *swadeshi* (self-sufficiency), and *sarvodaya* (uplift of all). That is why Gandhi's critique of Western education was part of his overall critique of modern civilization. His perception of the weakness of the West's focus on technical achievement became operative in what he presented as his "basic education," which laid emphasis on the harmonious development of the individual by further developing the best in a person. For Gandhi, basic education was supposed to help India move away from the Western concept of progress and toward a different form of development more suited to India's needs. The social philosophy of "basic education" favored two principal ideas: on the one hand, he saw it as a method for self-realization and personal development; on the other, it was necessary to prepare Indians for self-rule. In both senses, Gandhi saw education as a tool to empower the individual. He considered that empowered individuals were better equipped to question and critique societal realities and assumptions and more enabled to change their own situations. According to Gandhi, therefore, education implied both the transformation of institutions and the transformation of souls. He wished to train adults and children alike to be independent thinkers. Gandhi developed these ideas with the hope that his concept of basic education would become the basis of the national system. He did not mean simply the system of primary education, but the system from beginning to end. The system of basic education also aimed to improve the quality of life where one was born rather than encourage a "brain drain" to economic centers elsewhere. It aimed for the uplift of all, particularly women and girls. This uplift was not the task of a highly centralized state. That is to say, Gandhi viewed a state system of education as contradictory with the primary task of education, which was to make individuals autonomous and to change the established sociopolitical structures. According to Gandhi, children should realize from the beginning that being educated meant learning to share with others and being responsible toward society as a whole. Gandhi wanted to free Indian teachers from the slavery of bureaucracy and to elaborate a concept of learning that could not be fully implemented with the help of textbooks. He wrote: "If textbooks are treated as a vehicle for education, the living word of the teacher has very little value. A teacher who teaches from textbooks does not impart originality to his pupils."[28] There can be little doubt that, while writing these words, Gandhi was opting for a spiritual, as opposed to a purely professional, role for the teacher. Also, he was underlining the Indian motif of a guru-disciple relationship in an *ashram*. In such a community, the teacher was expected to set an example of an ethical life. In June 1938, he developed his views on this matter in speaking to a delegation of educators: "If the teacher himself lives up to the tenets of truth and justice, then alone can the children learn that Truth and Justice are the basis of all religions."[29] In other words, for Gandhi, true education should lead human beings to move away from their selfish egos and their false created needs and become more aware of their ethical and spiritual needs. Education, like much else in Gandhi's thought, is presented as a dynamic and open-ended experiment in truth and as a transformative process.

Gandhi believed that education should intensify the mutually reinforcing relationship between the political and the ethical. It was a key part of his broader effort to ethicalize Indian society and an investment in changing attitudes toward life. In characteristic Gandhian fashion, education was to aim at forging bonds of mutuality and awakening feelings of fellowship. It was a central part of the "constructive work," the acting and doing, which Gandhi took to be the natural and vital partner to "nonviolent resistance," with the latter's emphasis on refraining from action. Gandhi's Constructive

Program aimed to attain what Gandhi called *Poorna Swaraj* or complete independence by truthful and nonviolent means. This is to say that the promotion and consolidation of democratic governance and economic freedom are for Gandhi the two sides of the same coin. Gandhi observed that: "Democracy disciplined and enlightened is the finest thing in the world. A democracy prejudiced, ignorant, superstitious, will land itself in chaos and may be self-destroyed."[30] He understood that the line between democracy and mobocracy was often thin, and he knew well that Indians needed to become politically mature to be able to govern themselves. To do so they must embrace three interrelated values in particular: tolerance, nonviolence, and political solidarity. Gandhi knew that politics is not just a matter of mere policymaking. It is about debate and dialogue. It is about forging a collective ethics. For Gandhi, the answer to injustice, inequality, and oppression lay in a form of democracy built with the work of countless mature individuals, inspired by ethical commitments. He thought that "political life must be an echo of private life" and that "there cannot be any divorce between the two."[31]

Ultimately, if there is such a thing as "Gandhism," which Gandhi himself strongly repudiated, it appears like some kind of ethical imperative, holding within it a promise of pure politics. That is to say, Gandhi worked out his ethical imperative as spiritual praxis and understood that it had to evolve constantly in relation to the political community. As a combination of moral thought and political praxis, it was part of

Gandhi's success as a political leader and a universal moral voice to further the application of this dialogical approach to other social and cultural domains and finally to be able to find a global posterity for it. The course that the Gandhian spirit has taken along these lines since his assassination in 1948 has been difficult but fruitful. It seems to have inspired and brought to victory many civic struggles around the world.

CHAPTER FIVE

Gandhi's Reception in India

GANDHI AND HIS CRITICS

*Jinnah insists that Gandhi should admit that he is a
Hindu. Gandhi insists that Jinnah should admit that
he is one of the leaders of the Muslims. Never has there
been such a deplorable state of bankruptcy of states-
manship as one sees in these two leaders of India.*

DR. BABASAHEB AMBEDKAR

The dispute between Gandhi and Dr. B. R. Ambedkar is well
known to specialists on contemporary Indian history. However, what is not often mentioned by historians is that Gandhi
acknowledged Ambedkar as the most capable and talented representative of the Dalit group (untouchables) and that he per-
sonally intervened for Nehru to choose him as law minister
after independence.[1] Perhaps Gandhi did so, despite his disagreements with Ambedkar, because he believed in Ambedkar's
political capacities as a true freedom fighter and an integral

builder of democracy. Back in 1930, Ambedkar was a rising leader of the untouchables in the Indian public sphere as he led a direct action movement to allow the entry of *harijans* (Gandhi's term for untouchables) into the temple. Criticizing Gandhi for not making it a priority to end the caste system, Ambedkar accused Gandhi and Gandhians of strengthening Hindu domination in India. Asked about his critique of Gandhism and his ideas about social revolutions, Ambedkar explained: "Man has been waging war against nature and conquering her in order to be happier and happier and less and less handicapped. This process must go on until mankind becomes entirely happy and his poetic paradise is realized on earth. As I understand it, Gandhism is against this. Gandhism only wants to reduce man to the position of two bullocks he yokes to his plough, to shut up his women in the cottage to make her cook and procreate and ply on the charkha and deprive both of them of all cultures that can develop only by using the brain and mental faculties. This is Gandhism, which is wholly reactionary. Whatever movement Gandhi may start, its roots will be found in this line of thought and so Gandhi is not acceptable to me."[2] What Ambedkar points out here as unacceptable is the limit to which Gandhi would criticize castes. Gandhi certainly agreed that untouchables should be permitted into temples and had written extensively on the fate of the untouchables in 1920–1921 while explaining his religious position as a follower of Sanatan Dharma. But Gandhi's adherence to the spirit of the *Varna* system, which denied socioeconomic inequality and maintained hierarchy, is evident in his article in *Young India* written December 1920, where he affirms: "I believe that caste has saved Hinduism from disintegration. . . . But like every other institution it has suffered from excrescences. I consider the four divisions alone to be fundamental, natural, and essential. The innumerable subcasts are sometimes a convenience, after a hindrance. The sooner there is fusion the better. . . . But I am certainly against any attempt at destroying the fundamental divisions. The caste system is not based on inequality; there is no question of inferiority, and so far as there is any question arising, as in Madras, Maharashtra or elsewhere, the tendency should undoubtedly be checked."[3] This passage reflects Gandhi's adherence to the principle of *Varna*. It clearly implies his acceptance of the fusion among castes and his rejection of the Hindu orthodox reading of the caste society in India. However, as Christophe Jaffrelot underlines adequately, "Such a conception is naturally the exact opposite to that of Ambedkar, for whom the individual had to become the basic unit of an egalitarian society, with castes as collective bodies serving only as temporary means of advancing his politics of equality."[4]

Ambedkar was fully aware of the dangers of an independent India where there would be no share in political power for the depressed classes. He, therefore, expressed his disillusionment with a constitution that did not take into consideration the need for representation of the untouchables. It became obvious that Gandhi and Ambedkar's views could not be easily reconciled. Ambedkar did not take an extreme position, as did the Muslim League under Jinnah, to ask for a separate state, but he made it politically clear that he considered the untouchables a separate minority. Gandhi responded to Ambedkar's demand thusly: "Those who speak of the political rights of untouchables do not know their India, do not know how Indian society is today constructed, and therefore I want to say with all the emphasis that I can command that if I was the only person to resist this thing I would resist it with my life."[5] As a matter of fact, Gandhi distinguished between untouchability and *chaturvarna*, the system of four divisions. He believed that *chaturvarna* could exist without untouchability and that it did not necessitate inequality. As for Ambedkar, he advocated the total rejection of the *chaturvarnya* and accused Gandhi of being confused in his role as a Mahatma and as a politician: "As a Mahatma he may be trying to spiritualize politics. Whether he has succeeded in it or not, politics has certainly commercialized him. A politician must know that society cannot bear the whole truth and that he must not speak the whole truth; if he is speaking the whole truth it is bad for politics. The reason why the Mahatma is always supporting caste and *Varna* is because he is afraid that if he opposed them he will lose his place in politics. Whatever the source of his confusion, the Mahatma must be told that he is deceiving himself and also deceiving the people by preaching caste under the name of *Varna*."[6]

Gandhi's response to Ambedkar's severe critique of his political and religious stands was to make the abolition of untouchability central to his strategy of *swaraj* and to praise Ambedkar as a true *satyagrahi:* "The magnitude of [Dr. Ambedkar's] sacrifice is great. He is absorbed in his work. He leads a simple life. He is capable of earning one to two thousand rupees a month. He is also in a position to settle down in Europe if he so desires. But he doesn't want to stay there. He is only concerned about the welfare of the *Harijans*."[7] While Gandhi tried to conquer his opponent's heart, Ambedkar's utter dislike of the kind of leadership that Gandhi represented in relation to social issues became more and more evident. Ambedkar felt that Gandhi and the Congress Party were only conscious of the Muslim minority and none other. His book *What Congress and Gandhi have done to the Untouchables*, published in 1945, is a direct critique of Gandhi's policies with respect to the problem of the untouchables. The book is important because it covers a detailed examination of Gandhism as a social, economic, and political philosophy. Ambedkar tries to prove that Gandhism is not a suitable philosophy to a democratic society because it is "indifferent to machinery and the civilization based upon it." A few pages after writing this, Ambedkar argues: "That Mr. Gandhi changed over from the caste system to the *Varna* system does not make the slightest difference to the charge that Gandhism is opposed to democracy."[8]

That Gandhi had rejected caste might seem like progress, but Ambedkar was more concerned with Gandhi's approach to the two concepts of civilization and democracy. Ambedkar believed that to criticize modern civilization and simultaneously support a participative democracy was contradictory. He consistently emphasized the modern concept of "rights" in civic and political life, and, unlike Gandhi, he refused to get involved in questions of ethics and spirituality. Indeed, the main object of Ambedkar's life was not spirituality, but politics, which he considered as a means to uplift the situation of the depressed classes in India. He, therefore, came to the conclusion that there was no salvation for the untouchables within the framework of Hinduism. As a result of this, he declared: "Though I was born a Hindu, I do not intend to die a Hindu."[9] Eventually, he converted to Buddhism.

Ambedkar once remarked that what Gandhi had learned from history was that "Mahatmas, like fleeting fantoms raise dust, but raise no level."[10] What Ambedkar underestimated in Gandhi's political work was that the Mahatma was trying to put an end to the power of British in India while ending caste inequality and establishing communal harmony. To claim, however, as it is usually done, that Gandhi had a final solution for the caste problem in India would be far from being exact. Gandhi's political and spiritual intervention was doubtlessly important, insofar as it helped greatly to raise awareness among the Hindus about the unjust system of caste in India. But Gandhi did not find the opportunity to be drawn into parallel negotiations with Ambedkar as was the case with Jinnah and the Muslim League. His response to Ambedkar on August 6, 1944, reveals the level of his difficulty: "On broad politics of the country we see things from different angles. I would love to find a meeting ground between us. . . . I know your great ability and I would love to own you as a colleague and co-worker. But I must admit my failure to come nearer to you. If you can show me a way to a common meeting ground between us, I would like to see it. Meanwhile, I must reconcile myself to the present unfortunate difference."[11] The passage shows clearly that Gandhi did not reject all forms of dialogue with Ambedkar and his other critics. As a matter of fact, Gandhi was not only troubled by the attacks by Ambedkar on the one hand, and by the orthodox Hindus on the other, he was also perplexed by the view of those Indian Muslims who refused any attempts to achieve Hindu-Muslim unity. According to Rajmohan Gandhi, "Men like Savarkar, as well as sanatanists opposed to Gandhi over caste, attacked Gandhi as not being Hindu enough. Yet Jinnah insisted on seeing him and the Congress as exclusively Hindu."[12] To all those groups and individuals Gandhi reiterated his belief that in India religious pluralism and communal harmony went hand in hand and that they both be improved through the democratic life of the Indian nation after the independence. Gandhi, however, never contemplated achieving unity among the Hindus and the Muslims, or any solution to the problem of the untouchables, through the use of violence. It goes without saying that seeking Hindu-Muslim unity was a journey of trial and error for Gandhian nonviolence.

From the beginning of his *satyagraha* movement, Gandhi tried to gain Muslim adherence to the drive for India's self-rule.

To that end, in March 1918, he contacted the viceroy and urged him to release the Ali Brothers, two prominent Islamic leaders, from internment. In a letter to Muhammad Ali, Gandhi wrote: "My interest in your release is quite selfish. We have a common goal, and I want to utilize your services to the uttermost in order to reach that goal. In the proper solution of the Mohamedan question lies the realization of *swarajya*."[13] The alliance between Gandhi and the Indian Muslims was, however, full of misunderstandings and difficulties from the first days of the nonviolent movement. The Ali Brothers had also adopted the *satyagraha* in their own way, but not all Muslims agreed with Gandhi to adhere to nonviolence in all circumstances. Jinnah was among the Muslim leaders of the Congress Party who in 1915 welcomed Gandhi on his return from South Africa, but disagreements over Gandhi's Non-Cooperation campaign of 1920–1922 began what would be a long history of divergence between the two men. Jinnah, whose opposition to Gandhi's noncooperation was well-known to the British and to other members of the Congress Party, was especially perplexed by the fact that by 1920, the congress, like most of Muslim India, had accepted Gandhi as their charismatic leader. "Your methods have already caused split and division in almost every institution that you have approached hitherto," proclaimed Jinnah, "and in the public life between Hindus and Hindus and Muslims and Muslims and even fathers and sons; people generally are all over the country and your extreme programme has for the moment struck the imagination mostly of the inexperienced youth and the ignorant and the illiterate. All this means complete disorganization and chaos. What the consequence of this may be, I shudder to contemplate. . . . I do not wish my countrymen to be dragged to the brink of a precipice in order to be shattered."[14]

It is true that Gandhi's Congress-Khilafat noncooperation movement was partly responsible for Jinnah's skepticism and bitterness, but it goes also without saying that Jinnah's political style and the exaggerated "Britishness," which he adopted in his private and public life, left him little opportunity to compete with Gandhi's simplicity and transparency. It is absolutely clear that Jinnah's dream of an independent India did not go hand in hand with the Hindu-Muslim unity. Generally speaking, though Jinnah pleaded for the Muslim cause before the congress and the Hindu community through the years 1916 to 1938, he gradually gave up the idea of Hindu-Muslim unity and advocated the exclusive cause of Muslim India in the decade before Independence. Jinnah's correspondence with Pandit Nehru in 1938 bears clear testimony to the dead end that Jinnah had reached in his dealings with some of the leaders of the congress. For Gandhi, the questions of Indian home rule and Hindu-Muslim unity were not separate issues, whereas for Jinnah the opposite was true, as he told Gandhi: "We maintain and hold that Muslims and Hindus are two major nations by any definition or test of a nation. We are a nation of a hundred million, and what is more, we are a nation with our own distinctive culture and civilization, language and literature, art and architecture, names and nomenclature, sense of values and proportion, legal laws and moral codes, customs and calendar, history and traditions, aptitudes and ambitions, in short we have our own distinctive outlook on life and of life. By all canons of international law we are a nation."[15]

Jinnah strongly resented linking the *swaraj* movement to the Khilafat movement that Indian Muslims founded after World War I to press the cause of Muslims in the Ottoman Empire. Jinnah was, in the words of Durga Das, "Amazed that the Hindu leaders had not realized that this movement would encourage the Pan-Islamic sentiment."[16] Gandhi, however, saw in Khilafat an opportunity to seek Muslim cooperation in the *swaraj* movement. His political intentions in doing so were more democratic than theocratic. It would be wrong, therefore, to underline, as some analysts of Indian contemporary political history do, that Gandhi was "unwittingly responsible for jettisoning sane, secular, modernist leadership among the Muslims of India and foisting upon Indian Muslims, a theocratic orthodoxy of the Maulvis."[17] Jinnah, like Ambedkar, criticized Gandhi's insistence on the spiritualization of Indian politics. He was against Gandhi's view of bringing religious issues into the public sphere because he considered it disastrous and irrelevant for political matters. Jinnah himself, however, prioritized religion and was considered a "communalist" by many of his critics.[18] In his long political career, Jinnah clearly perceived Indian self-determination from the perspective of the Muslim community. As for Gandhi, it was quite the opposite. Ever since his first writings in South Africa, Gandhi replaced the divisive view of religion by a pluralist and tolerant one by equating religion with ethics. This, of course, was how Gandhi reacted against the specter of the "Hindu raj" and the cries of "Islam is in danger" that widened the communal gulf in India and created a climate of hatred. For Gandhi, the difference between the Hindus and the Muslims was not confined to religion. It was due, according to him, to the lack of truthfulness and transparency in the political realm. As a social reformer, Gandhi believed strongly in the affinity between spirituality and politics, and it is not surprising that he chose to work with people whose primary interests were best defined in spiritual and ethical terms. He once declared that a true Muslim could not harm a Hindu, and a true Hindu could not harm a Muslim.[19] It was probably in this spirit that Gandhi developed a friendship with and a great esteem for the Islamic leaders Maulana Azad and Khan Abdul Ghaffar Khan. In 1939, during his third visit to Ghaffar Khan, Gandhi proclaimed: "If you dissect my heart, you will find that the prayer and spiritual striving for the attainment of Hindu-Muslim unity goes on there unceasingly all the twenty-four hours without even a moment's interruption whether I am awake or asleep. . . . The dream [of Hindu-Muslim unity] has filled my being since the earliest childhood."[20]

It is true that Gandhi was influenced by the tolerant Islam of Ghaffar Khan and Maulana Azad and their "soft reading" of the Qur'an, but it is also true that the spiritual teachings of the

Mahatma and his political pragmatism captivated the minds of these two men. Unlike Gandhi's critics, both Azad and Ghaffar Khan understood the Gandhian philosophical principle of an "acid test of reason," which he applied to every formula of everyday politics and religion. This principle helped them to reformulate Islam and Indian politics in accord with the philosophical foundations of nonviolence.

THINKING A GANDHIAN ISLAM

Mutual respect for one another's religions is inherent in a peaceful society.

MAHATMA GANDHI

Some years ago, the famous Catholic theologian Hans Kung said: "There can be no peace between the nations until there is peace between the religions. There can be no peace between the religions until there is dialogue between the religions."[21] Gandhi would have readily supported such a statement. Gandhi believed all religions were equal because, according to him, at the core of every religion were truth and love. He had the same regard for other faiths as he had for his own because he believed such respect would not only remove religious rifts but also lead to the realization that religion in general was a stabilizing force, not a source of discord. Gandhi's basic axiom was that the scriptures of all religions point in only one direction: to the quest for truth. For him, truth was far more important and more powerful than any religion itself. That is why he was critical of the hypocrisy in organized religion, rather than the principles on which they were based. According to Gandhi, truth as God lives within us. It is that little voice that tells us what to do, but also guides the universe. Gandhi's "inner voice" is the equivalent of Socrates's "daimon," an authority higher than the laws of the land. "For me," said Gandhi, "the voice of God, of Conscience, of Truth or the Inner Voice . . . mean one and the same thing. . . . For me, the voice was more real than my own existence. It has never failed me, and for that matter, anyone else."[22] As Gandhi said often during his campaigns, the inner voice was for him an authority higher than the laws of the land. From a spiritual perspective, of course, the experience of hearing a call or voice meant for Gandhi that he found deep inside him an inner sanctuary of the soul. Gandhi learned how to live in this world by listening to his inner voice. It helped him cultivate the kind of emotional, spiritual, and moral intelligence he needed to make life choices that were suited to who he was and who he was called to become.

Furthermore, Gandhi referred to the inner voice as a soul force that has the power to elicit the divine in us so that religion is not simply the mechanical following of the dictates of organized religion. This voice would affirm our commitment to nonviolence, since its compassionate quality would lead us to a dialogical exchange with the self and the others. The inner voice might be described as a kind of spiritual insight that enhances one's sense of how to distinguish good and the evil.

That is to say, one is invited to action by one's inner voice rather than compelled to act in response to the external environment. One thing to keep in mind, which many supporters seem to forget, is that Gandhi was a normal human like you and me. He made mistakes just like every other man, but he had the courage to always follow his inner voice even in his imperfections. It was this that made Gandhi such a formidable political actor. His commitment to nonviolence was not just a political tactic, but a deep form of spirituality.

Gandhi's mission was not to politicize religion, but to spiritualize politics, meaning to bind up everyday action in the public sphere with morality. Gandhi believed religion and politics should creatively comingle and not remain separate entities. He believed that ethical and spiritual values must underlie daily politics, and indeed it was Gandhi's spirituality that drew him into politics in the first place. Gandhi's *Autobiography* provides us with vital information about his views here. According to Gandhi, "To see the universal and all-pervading spirit of Truth face to face one must be able to love the meanest of creation as oneself. And a man who aspires after that cannot afford to keep out of any field of life. That is why my devotion to Truth has drawn me into the field of politics; and I can say without the slightest hesitation and yet in all humility that those who say that religion has nothing to do with politics do not know what religion means."[23] One might argue that Gandhi's primary contribution to spirituality is nonviolence. This was how he challenged people of faith to recognize their religious hypocrisies. Gandhi argued that a person who believes in truth and God cannot go to a mosque, synagogue, temple, or church one day and the next day foster hatred and violence. Thus for Gandhi the spirituality of nonviolence had to be applied to all facets of life. It is interesting to see how much Gandhi was able to influence believers of other religions by unlocking the spiritual dynamic in all of them. Through his "soft reading" of the Hindu scriptures, and also those of Christianity and Islam, Gandhi found a clarion call to active nonviolence in all these religions. As such, he taught Christians, Jews, and Muslims that faith pushes us to promote peace and nonviolent social change. For him, the basic principles of religions were not just pious ideals, but actual laws of action in the world. Maybe this is why Gandhi challenged fervent believers of different religions to seek God through their own active pursuit of truth and nonviolence instead of being literalist interpreters of the Hindu, Muslim, or Christian scriptures.

Gandhi knew that independence could not come about by the efforts of Hindus alone. He made it a priority to involve Indian Muslims in the struggle. Discontent with the "us-and-them" divisions and mutual antipathy between Muslims and Hindus, Gandhi engaged in an open dialogue with Islam and Muslims. He never accepted the argument that Hindus and Muslims constituted two separate elements in Indian society. His willingness to go out of his way to win over Muslims to the congress won him many Islamic friends and admirers, not least because his attitude was so different from that of some other prominent nationalists. From its very beginning, India's national struggle had three divisions: secular, Hindu, and Muslim. Such early nationalists as Aurobindo Ghosh, together with Bal Gangadhar Tilak and Lala Lajpat Rai, constituted an "extremist" core within the Indian National Congress. Tilak was instrumental in shaping Hindu nationalism. He took a prominent part in inflaming the minds of Hindus against the Muslims. He was accused of inciting the Hindus to assert their rights to play music in passing before mosques. He even called the Muslims savage, claiming that "even a savage race like the Mohammedans did not disarm the Hindus while exercising their imperial sway over India."[24] Tilak at least compares Muslims favorably with the British in this comment, which points to the possibility of an anticolonialist alliance of some kind between Hindus and Muslims, but it is hardly a gesture of fellowship. For that, the nationalist movement needed Gandhi, and of course it needed Muslims who would engage with him in return. Prominent among the Muslims who worked with Gandhi in a complementary spirit of generosity and pluralism were his companions, Maulana Abul Kalam Azad and Khan Abdul Ghaffar Khan.

Very few deeply religious people show the daring and courage to criticize their own dogmatism and turn against their prejudices. Among the leading Muslims who have left a deep impact on the idea of pluralism in Islam, Maulana Azad stands out in part because he was so willing to question himself. He will not only be remembered in the history of India for his role in the national liberation movement, but also for standing for dialogue between Muslims and Hindus, this despite his early career as a fundamentalist. Azad eventually came to be known as "the Muslim on whom Gandhi relied for advice" and was "a prominent example of the communal inclusiveness of Congress."[25] It was not a position that he always seemed destined to hold.

Maulana Azad was born in Mecca in 1888. His father, Maulana Khairuddin, was a pious man who had married an Arab woman by the name of Aliyah, the daughter of Mohammad Zaher Watri, an Arabic scholar from Medina. Maulana Azad lived in Mecca with his parents until the age of ten. In 1908, he traveled to Turkey, Egypt, Syria, and France. In Mecca, Azad learned the fundamentals of the Qur'an and of Arabic. He spoke Arabic with his mother and Urdu with his father. Azad's mother died a year after they settled in Calcutta in 1898. At fourteen, Azad was writing poetry in Urdu and had his first experiences of journalism with the journal/magazine *Khadang-e Nazr* of Lucknow. The writings of Sir Sayyid Ahmad Khan, commonly known as Sir Sayyid, an Indian educator and politician and an Islamic reformer and modernist, deeply influenced Azad during his teenage years. It was under Sir Sayyid's influence that Azad learned English and studied philosophy and science. "Sir Sayyid also stimulated the boy's interest in certain aspects of his Islamic heritage that had not been emphasized in his training at home, among them the history of Mu'tazalites, the early rationalist sect that provided the source of many of Sir Sayyid's ethical ideas."[26] Although Sir Sayyid influenced Azad at this stage of his life, others also made an impression. He first had contact with Christian missionaries during the family's second move to Bombay in 1904. It was also during this time that Azad got a glimpse of political activism in India through the Swadeshi Movement in Bengal. "He was impressed by the revolutionaries' activities, and claimed to have joined one of their groups through the mediation of Shyam Sunder Chakravarty, an associate of Aurobindo Ghose."[27]

Azad started his career in politics and activism as a revivalist Muslim and as an upholder of pure Islam. His early career from 1906 to 1920 was influenced by his religious teachings. During this period, Azad firmly believed that the Muslims were the leaders of the world. In his early writings and speeches, which appeared in his journal *Al-Hilal*, Azad talked about the superiority of Muslims over the followers of other religions and called for an "Islamic Way" to independence. In these writings, he appeared as a Muslim fundamentalist who favored a close relationship between politics and religion. His response to a correspondent of *Al-Hilal* in the December 29, 1921, issue characterizes his fundamentalist tone in those days. "You have suggested separation of politics from religion," underlined Azad in his article. "But if we do this what, then, is left with us? We have developed our political thinking from religion. . . . We believe that every thought which draws inspiration from any institution (including politics) other than the Quran is *Kufr* (infidelity)."[28] After 1920, he underwent a radical change, ceasing to be a revivalist Muslim and instead embracing Indian secular nationalism as a political philosophy. Without a doubt the evolution of Azad's outlook from Pan-Islamic to secular nationalist was determined by his friendship and collaboration with Mahatma Gandhi and by the rise of the communal problems in the Indian liberation movement. Through Gandhi, Azad came to see how central communal harmony would be to the future of an independent India. In spite of religious, ethnic, and linguistic differences, he believed that India was one nation. Azad saw that the "two-nation theory" offered "no solution of the problem of one another's minorities, but only lead to retribution and reprisals by introducing a system of mutual hostages."[29] Like Gandhi, Azad considered Hindu-Muslim unity as a necessary principle for the national reconstruction of India. In his famous address to the Agra session of the Khalifat Conference on August 25, 1921, he referred to Hindu-Muslim unity as a moral imperative for India's future. He proclaimed: "If the Muslims of India would like to perform their best religious and Islamic duties . . . then they must recognize that it is obligatory for the Muslims to be together with their Hindu brethren . . . and it is my belief that the Muslims in India cannot perform their best duties, until in conformity within the injunctions of Islam, in all honesty, they establish unity and cooperation with the Hindus. This belief is based on the imperative spirit of Islam."[30] Azad aimed to show Muslims that the fundamental teaching of the Qur'an is mercy and forgiveness (*rahmat*). Therefore, it followed for him that these attributes of God should also be followed by human beings. It is interesting to see up to what point Azad's *tafsir* (interpretation) of the Qur'an keeps its closeness to the text and to what extent it is inspired by the Sufi perception of God through *kashf* (personal revelation). Azad's faith in the essential unity of humanity and in the oneness of all religions stemmed essentially from the Sufi concept of "the unity of existence" (*wahdat-i-wujud*). Truth, for Azad, was one and the same everywhere. The mistake was to equate particular forms of truth with truth itself. Read with this in mind, Azad's most important book, *Tarjuman-ul-Qur'an*, illustrates his firm belief in tolerance and dialogue. In this book Azad powerfully expresses his idea of religious pluralism through the concept of the oneness of faiths (*wahdat-i-Din*). For Azad, God as the "cherisher" and "nourisher" (*Rabb*) transcends all fragmentations and divisions of humanity in race, color, and religion. The path of universal God (*Rabb-ul-Alameen*) is "the right path" (*Sirat-al-Mustaqeem*), which belongs to no particular religion. In one of his celebrated works entitled *Ghubar-i-Khatir*, Azad drew a parallel between the Sufi concept of the "unity of existence" and the idea of pantheism as formulated in the Hindu *Upanishads*. If, at root, all religions reflected the same message, then, for Azad, there was no room for Hindu or Muslim communalism. As a champion of Indian nationalism and democracy, Azad sought a synthesis of modern secularism and spiritual traditionalism. He took his stand upon truth by unifying the soul of Islam with the glory of his nation. "I am a Muslim and this fills me with pride," he proclaimed in his presidential address in 1942 at Ramgarh. "But in addition to these feelings, I am also the possessor of another, which has been created by the stark realities of my external life. The soul of Islam is not a barrier to this belief; in fact, it guides me in this path. I am proud to be an Indian."[31] To achieve Indian solidarity, Azad thought, Indians had to overcome religious nationalism and communalism. He believed the answer was to embrace a secular nationalism that made room for all of India's religions. To the extent that religious communalism stood in the way of secular democracy, he thought it was an obstacle to deep pluralism.

Nonviolence was a key component of Azad's secular nationalism. He held that a commitment to dialogue among faiths and the spirit of peace were both characteristic of Islam. He believed, moreover, that nonviolence was an effective strategy in the struggle for independence. Unlike Gandhi, Azad did not believe in nonviolence as an article of faith, but only as a matter of policy. According to him, nonviolence was not a moral absolute, but an expedient principle. He was, however, resolutely opposed to committing violence for religious reasons. In light of his religious humanism, Azad stated that there was no justification whatsoever for imposing one religion on another because the fundamentals of religions (*Din*) were one. Every individual had a right to follow his own religious path. Azad viewed religion from the wider perspective of a universal humanist, and his philosophy was free from any form of religious narrowness and dogma. It is in relation with this aspect of Azad's thought that the comment of India's President Zakir Husain, resonates. "In my opinion," said Zakir Husain, "the greatest service which the Maulana did was to teach people of every religion that there are two aspects of religion. One separates and creates hatred. This is the false aspect. The other, the true spirit of religion, brings people together; it creates understanding. It lies in the spirit of service, in sacrificing self for others. It implies belief in unity, in the essential unity of things."[32] Azad owed his political inspiration to his knowledge of Islam. But as a defender of shared common values, he believed that religions were the common heritage of all mankind. His increasing receptivity to the message of other faiths led him to the recognition of the humanist element in religion. This is why for him the outward forms of religion were useless without moral actions. From his point of view, religion was not supposed to dictate specific political actions but to mold one's general principles in life. This is how Azad grew beyond the revivalism of his *Al-Hilal* period to apply a deeper spirituality, as a moral imperative, to politics. His awareness of other religions also encouraged him to promote the idea of a humanist coexistence of faiths. Azad's universal humanism led him on to fiercely oppose Muslim and Hindu communalism, which saw no place for a genuine religiously plural and democratic independent India. His plea for religious humanism and communal harmony was directly influenced by his political affinities with Gandhi and his mystical reading of Islam. Azad believed unity between Muslims and Hindus was necessary for the independence movement to succeed: "He believed that constitutional forms could be devised for India in which the two communities could both thrive. He seems to have opted to follow Gandhi for much the same reason that most of the South African Muslims had done, namely that the Hindu activist seemed the most effective leader available in the struggle against white racism and brutal imperialism. It was Gandhi's ability as an effective fighter that drew Azad to him."[33]

Gandhi had a sense of brotherhood with Muslims. We should not forget that he traveled to South Africa in 1893 to work as a lawyer for a Muslim firm. The Hindu-Muslim unity that Gandhi experienced in South Africa not only confirmed his past experiences with Muslim friends as an adolescent in Gujarat, but also provided him with a new vision of Islam and its civilizational signification in India. In an address to the Congress Working Committee in 1942, he reiterated the importance of these issues: "Hindu-Muslim unity is not a new thing. Millions of Hindus and Musulmans have sought after it. I consciously strove for its achievement from my boyhood. While at school, I made it a point to cultivate the friendship of Muslim and Parsi co-students. I believed even at that tender age that the Hindus in India, if they wished to live in peace and amity with the other communities, should assiduously cultivate the virtue of neighborliness."[34] This passage is a telling example of the way in which Gandhi spontaneously took to using Hindu-Muslim unity in the context of his struggle for independence. Gandhi often used the Qur'an at the same level as the *Gita* or the *Ramayana* as an important text in shaping his religious consciousness. He even equated the struggle of the Prophet Muhammad with the mythical struggle of Rama against Ravana. Indeed, it seems that Gandhi's personal interest in Islam was partly due to his fascination with the character of the Prophet Muhammad. He read and translated Washington Irving's *Life of Muhammad*, but was also introduced to the firm, vigorous, and courageous character of the prophet by reading Thomas Carlyle's *Heroes and Hero Worship*. Gandhi wrote: "My religion says that only he who is prepared to suffer can pray to God. Fasting and prayer are common injunctions in my religion. But I know of this sort of penance even in Islam. In the life of the Prophet, I have read that the Prophet often fasted and prayed and forbade others to copy him. Someone asked him why he did not allow others to do things he himself was doing. 'Because I live on food divine,' he said. He achieved most of his great things by fasting and prayer. I learnt from him that only he can fast who has inexhaustible faith in God."[35] Gandhi's admiration for the Prophet Muhammad and his understanding of a tolerant Islam were strengthened by his reading of Azad's commentary on the Qur'an. He came to believe that nonviolence had deep roots in Islam. "Though, in my opinion, nonviolence had a predominant place in the Qur'an, the thirteen hundred years of imperialistic expansion made the Mussalmans fighters as a body. They are, therefore, aggressive. Bullying is the natural excrescence of an aggressive spirit. . . . I refuse to be lifted off my feet because of the scares that haunt us today. If Hindus would but believe in themselves and work in accordance with their traditions, they will have no reason to fear bullying. The moment they recommence the real spiritual training, the Mussalman will respond. He cannot help. If I can get together a band of young Hindus with faith in themselves, and, therefore, a faith in the Mussalmans, the band will become a shield for the weaker ones."[36]

No less important to Gandhi's conception of Islam was his friendship and empathic partnership with Khan Abdul Ghaffar Khan. While Azad introduced Gandhi to a Sufi understanding of Islam, Ghaffar Khan introduced him to the practical and pragmatic virtues of nonviolent Islam. Khan was born in 1890 at Utmanzai, a district of Peshawar. He was the fourth child of Bahram Khan, a landowner of Mohammadzai clan. Ghaffar Khan was sent to the local mosque to take early Qur'anic lessons. Later he was sent to the Municipal Board High School at Peshawar and soon after joined Edwardes Memorial Mission High School at Peshawar. Ghaffar Khan summarized later in his autobiography the experience he had with this mission school. "While in school," he wrote, "there awoke in my heart a great love for my country and my people and a strong desire to serve my country and my community."[37] He was initially encouraged by a family servant to join the British Indian Army. Yet an incident with a British Raj officer changed his mind, and he decided to continue his studies. But his father's decision to send him to England to study alongside his brother, Khan

Sahib, was put off after his mother's intervention. Ghaffar Khan instead began work on various social causes and joined a group of Pashtoon intellectuals, including Maulvi Fazl-i-Rabi, Maulvi Taj Mohammad, and Fazal Mahmood Makhfi. In 1913, Abdul Ghaffar Khan joined the Annual Session of the All-India Muslim League in Agra and was deeply impressed by Maulana Kalam Azad. This event marked his debut in politics. Subsequently, he organized a meeting at Utmanzai to protest against the Rowlatt Act enforced by the British Raj. He was immediately arrested and imprisoned for six months. He then joined the Khilafat Movement and established closed contacts with the Ali brothers, who had aligned themselves with Gandhi. On April 1, 1921, Ghaffar Khan formed the *Anjuman-i-Islah-ul-Afaghana* (the Society for the Reformation of Afghans). Nine days later he instituted the first branch of *Azad Islamia Madrassa*. The curriculum in the school included teaching of the Qur'an, Islamic history, Pashto, mathematics, English, and Arabic. During the same year, Ghaffar Khan was invited by the provincial Khilafat Committee at Peshawar to become its president. He was subsequently arrested and sentenced to three years rigorous imprisonment. In the process he suffered solitary confinement and torture, but he was finally released in 1924 and received a warm welcome back from the Pashtoons. In late 1928, events in Afghanistan and the abdication of King Amanullah Khan in favor of a British-supported bandit called Habibullah made the Pashtoon tribes indignant. A large meeting of Pashtoon leaders was convened in Utmanzai in

1929, and Ghaffar Khan announced the creation of an organization by the name of Khudai Khidmatgars, Servants of God, which became a major force of 50,000 men and women who would dress distinctively in brick-red shirts. The most significant feature of the Khudai Khidmatgars was their discipline and adherence to nonviolence. The volunteers were taught not to carry weapons and to oppose any kind of blood feuds and factionalism. Ghaffar Khan explained this fact in his *Autobiography:* "The Pathans used to quarrel amongst themselves; antagonism and feuds ruined their homes and their families. Through nonviolent movement all that was changed. The British used to say, 'a nonviolent Pathan is more dangerous than a violent Pathan.' "[38] It is interesting to underline that membership in the Khudai Khidmatgars was kept open to all, irrespective of caste, community, or religion. In 1931, the Khudai Khidmatgars was formally federated with the congress. Ghaffar Khan proved himself to be a firm believer in nonviolence and served as host when Gandhi visited the Pashtoon country in May 1938.

Ghaffar Khan had convinced Gandhi that Muslims were capable of practicing nonviolence in politics and in advocating social reforms. Gandhi in turn was a true inspiration to Ghaffar Khan and his "Red Shirts" in their practice of nonviolence among the Pashtoons. But Ghaffar Khan's profound belief in the truth and effectiveness of nonviolence came also from the depths of his personal experience of Islam. For him, Islam was selfless service, faith, and love. And he underlined that "without these one calling himself a Muslim is like a sounding brass and tinkling cymbal."[39] Just as Gandhi considered Hinduism to be based on nonviolent ahimsa, so Abdul Ghaffar Khan reinterpreted his Islam to be based on nonviolence. For both reformers, systematic nonviolent social transformation was a matter of faith. "My non-violence has almost become a matter of faith with me," explained Ghaffar Khan. "I believed in Gandhi's ahimsa long before. But the unparalleled success of the experiment in my province has made me a confirmed champion of nonviolence. . . . Surely there is nothing surprising in a Muslim or a Pathan like me subscribing to this creed. It is not a new creed. It was followed fourteen hundred years ago by the Prophet, all the time he was in Mecca. And it has since been followed by all those who wanted to throw off the oppressor's yoke. But we had so far forgotten it that when Mahatma Gandhi placed it before us, we thought that he was sponsoring a new creed or a novel weapon."[40]

Many factors contributed to the popularity of the Khudai Khidmatgars. Different sections of the Pashtoon society interpreted its program in their own way. "To the Pashtoon intelligentsia, it was a movement for the revival of Pashtoon culture with its distinct identity. To the smaller Khans, it was a movement that demanded political reforms for the province that would enfranchise them and give them a greater role in the governance. Its anti-colonial stand suited the majority of the anti-establishment *Ulema*, who always regarded British rule in the subcontinent as a 'curse.' For the peasants and other poor

classes it was against their economic oppressors, British imperialism and its agents the pro-British Nawabs, Khan Bahadurs
and the big Khans."[41] Ghaffar Khan's truthful character and
his faithful and principled method of practicing nonviolence
convinced the Pashtoons that the only panacea for their blood
feuds and factionalism was adoption of nonviolence and strict
adherence to it. According to J. S. Bright, a contemporary
biographer of Ghaffar Khan:

> Ghaffar Khan is in complete accord with the principle
> of non-violence. But he has not borrowed his outlook
> from Mahatma Gandhi. He has reached it and reached
> it independently. Independently like a struggler after
> truth. No doubt, his deep study of Koran has influ-
> enced his doctrine of love. . . . Hence if Ghaffar Khan
> has arrived at the philosophy of non-violence, it is
> absolutely no wonder. Of the two, Ghaffar Khan and
> Mahatma Gandhi, my personal view is that the former
> has achieved a higher level of spirituality. The Khan
> has reached heaven, while the Pandit is firmly on the
> earth but ironically enough, the Mahatma is strug-
> gling in the air! Ghaffar Khan, like Shelley, has come
> from heaven to the earth, while Mahatma Gandhi, like
> Keats, is going from earth to the heaven. Hence, I do
> not understand why Ghaffar Khan should be called
> the Frontier Gandhi. There is no other reason except
> this that the Mahatma was earlier in the field, more

ambitious than spiritual, and has been able to capture, somehow or the other, a greater publicity. If we judge a person by spiritual qualities, Mahatma Gandhi should rather be called the Indian Khan than Ghaffar Khan the Frontier Gandhi: true, there the matter ends.[42]

Because of his proximity to Gandhi, Ghaffar Khan was accused by some of his close associates including Mian Ahmad Shah, Abdul Akbar Khan Akbar, and Mohammad Akbar Khadim of subordinating the Khudai Khidmatgars with the Hindu-dominated congress. Ghaffar Khan's response to his Pathan critics and to his future colleagues in the Indian Congress Party was the following: "I should like to make it clear that the non-violence I have believed in and preached to my brethren of the *Khudai Khidmatgars* is much wider. It affects all our life, and only this has permanent value. Unless we learn this lesson of non-violence fully we shall never do away with the deadly feuds which have been the curse of the people of the Frontier. Since we took to non-violence and the *Khudai Khidmatgars* pledged them to it, we have largely succeeded in ending these feuds. Non-violence has added greatly to the courage of the Pathans. Because they were previously addicted to violence far more than others, they have profited by non-violence much more. We shall never really and effectively defend ourselves except through non-violence. *Khudai Khidmatgars* must, there-fore, be what our names imply pure servants of God and humanity by laying down our own lives and never taking any life."[43] Gandhi's response to this was as clear as always, confirming his belief in the nonviolent essence of Islam. "I do not know how far the Khan Sahib has succeeded in carrying his message to his people," wrote Gandhi, "[But] this I know that with him nonviolence is a matter not of intellectual conviction but of intuitive faith. Nothing can therefore shake it. About his followers he cannot say how far they will adhere to it. But that does not worry him. He has to do his duty which he owes to them. The result he leaves to God. He derives his ahimsa from the Holy Quran."[44] One could certainly argue that Ghaffar Khan succeeded as much as Mahatma Gandhi in his practice of nonviolent action, when he turned the hardy Pathans toward nonviolence and away from the customary rough methods they often used to settle their disputes with the government and among themselves. Of course, neither Maulana Azad nor Abdul Ghaffar Khan ultimately succeeded in convincing Muhammad Ali Jinnah to cease calling for the creation of Pakistan, a process that precipitated great violence for Muslims and Hindus alike. But this simply illustrates how Islam has always been used for both nonviolent and violent purposes. There is no denying that the life stories of Ghaffar Khan and Maulana Azad epitomize the challenges that Muslims have faced in grappling with violence and nonviolence and prove that nonviolent action could be consistent with Islamic principles. If imaginative Muslim leaders today could draw upon the nonviolent contributions of individuals like Ghaffar Khan and Maulana Azad, even in contexts where violent reactions may seem justified, tensions among religious or ethnic communities might be managed with far less danger for the human race.

Today, Islam and Muslims are largely portrayed in much of the world as synonymous with terrorism. There is a stereotypical view that Islam and nonviolence cannot coexist. Many Westerners, when they think of Islam, probably do not think of nonviolence, but rather of "Islamic terrorists" going on suicide bombing raids or of "Islamic extremists" blowing up planes and buildings. The events of September 11, 2001, led to an insistent linkage between violence and Islam. However, history offers much evidence of Muslim tolerance and civil engagement with other faiths and cultural traditions. Córdoba has become a byword for the pluralism of the *convivencia* in which Christians, Jews, and Muslims fostered a thriving civilization in Andalusia. While far from perfect, pluralist Muslim rule there between the eighth and fifteenth centuries was in advance of the rest of Europe well into the early modern period. The truth is that in Islam, as in other great religions, there are fundamentalists and extremists who manipulate what is written in their holy book to justify acts of violence and terrorism. Modern fundamentalism presented itself as a form of resistance to the secular and atheist world by launching a campaign against the symbols of modernity, including commercial buildings, train stations, and subways. It is the right time for liberal and moderate Muslims to construct a new image of Islam as a religion that is compatible with the modern world and whose practitioners are able to interact with the West and coordinate themselves with international norms. It is in the interest of Islamic societies and Muslims in general to change the world's perception of Islam as a violent religion by changing the way in which their societies often attempt to solve differences among themselves and with others. This is not a way to be hypocritical or to underestimate the civilizational potential of Islam, but it is a critical attitude to adopt to improve social and political conditions within Islam. Very often, Muslims protest against these kinds of arguments. However, by using violence as a social and political *modus vivendi*, many Muslims put their moral judgments and philosophical arguments at the same level as what they allegedly criticize and reject as unjust and inhuman; and that puts them, by definition, at an equally low or even lower level of morality. And this is not a game to gamble on; in Muslim countries that have embraced violence against their citizens or others, the violation of individual liberties is a matter of daily practice. Most Muslim societies are stricken with the poverty, corruption, and social disparities that are endemic to the developing world. These frustrations express themselves in religious "fundamentalist" terms, as Islamist movements also tend to support social and political revolutions. The other dimension to "fundamentalist" movements is external rather than internal. Muslim fundamentalists perceive the West and its allies to be responsible for imperialist policies directed at politically and economically suppressing Muslim populations. Anger at these Western policies fuels religious extremism and regressive views of violence all over the Islamic world, which could effectively bring to silence nonviolent interpretations of Islam everywhere. Because there appears to be no effective responses to the suffering of the people in Iraq, Palestine, and Afghanistan, Muslim publics are easily convinced that violent strategies are the only solution. Those who suggest otherwise, unfortunately, lose public legitimacy.

Reading Gandhi as a problematizer of violence and modernity in Muslim countries today is to help promote nonviolence in these countries. Gandhi's harsh critiques of tradition and modernity offer a theoretical terrain for a nonviolent critique of violence in Muslim theology and political philosophy. To develop an Islamic approach to nonviolence that is dialogical and pluralistic, one needs to move beyond Western models of peace building and conflict resolution by building upon alternative models of peace and nonviolence. A return to figures such as Khan Abdul Ghaffar Khan and Maulana Azad means accepting Gandhi's invitation to self-examination and self-criticism. The results of such a process are certainly unpredictable, but given the Gandhian view that no one possesses the whole truth and that truth emerges in a dialogical encounter among subjects, the making of a new Muslim Gandhi in the twenty-first century remains an important challenge.

Today, political Islam is largely an ideological response to the hegemony that the West has acquired in our time. The success political Islam has enjoyed says much about the failure of the secular state in providing a space where democratic culture and faith traditions can both thrive—and its failure in capturing the Muslim public imagination. Postcolonial secular governments have often been aggressive in their projects of modernization and lacking in sensitivity toward religion and forcefully authoritarian in their politics. This does not mean that Muslim societies are somehow averse to democracy and pluralism, as the "clash of civilizations" thesis would have us believe. Inclusive governance and the rule of law have flourished before in Muslim societies—and they cannot, in any case, be imposed from above or outside, as contemporary Iraq has shown. For dialogical civil society to emerge as the space where pluralist democracy can take root, a shift is needed in the exercise of citizenship. That is, citizenship that is "antagonistic" in nature and prone to violence can give way to one that is more engaged in open and pluralistic dialogue, where citizens have an effective stake. Such a shift only happens when a society can come to grips with the need for a civic space that is also ethical. Indeed, a civic space without the binding fabric of shared ethical values is difficult to sustain. This is not about forsaking secular culture—which is what makes a dialogical ethical space more likely. Nor should secular culture mean the exclusion of the spiritual factor from the public sphere. It is here that the Gandhian narrative of "spiritualization of politics," which rejects fundamentalist violence in favor of a dialogical exchange between politics and religion, can take root. Gandhi resisted the claim that political modernity depends on the primacy of secular reason over spiritual narrative. The latter is not just a stock of historical ideas and longings. It is a lived experience for individuals and communities that cannot be reduced to secular fundamentalist and rational instrumentalist discourses without stripping away meaningful and ethical facets of civilizational identity. The stripping away of normative roots and ethical attachments too frequently leads to a greater readiness to embrace versions of modernity that are only about techno-scientific values and that have little of substance to say about deeper spiritual quests and solidarities.

It is interesting to examine how helpful Gandhi's "spiritualization of politics" can be in helping steer the Muslim public space away from state-dominated as well as other forms of political Islam, while contributing to genuine dialogical pluralism and ethical civicism. In enunciating his principle of nonviolence through such concepts as *ahimsa*, *satyagraha*, *swaraj*, and *sarvodaya*, Gandhi constantly challenged the classical paradigms of political and religious thinking by globalizing the forces of soul, truth, and love. Gandhi's pluralist reading of religion in general and Islam in particular was an attempt to provide religious thinking with spiritual and ethical capacities to overcome its own theocratic and authoritarian experiences. Gandhi's articulations on the question of Khalifat provide us with a clue to his civilizational approach to Islamic history as a geopolitical and geocultural space dominated and endangered by the colonial and capitalist enterprise. Gandhi's interest in the Khilafat movement could be considered as an instance of his interest in civilizational Islam, but also as a political strategy for bringing Indian Muslims into the anticolonial and anti-imperialist struggle. Initially, very few Muslims were involved in the Khalifat movement, and some did not share its convictions. Gandhi, however, was hoping to win the support of these Muslims by becoming one of the movement's organizers, but at the same time he was trying to take Indians' attention away from communal tensions by focusing on the spiritual and moral common grounds between the Muslims and the Hindus. Broadly, this reflected that the Gandhian approach to religion and its role in the public space is characterized by two visions: first, a picture of an ideal society that is summed up in the word *Rama Rajya*, the "Kingdom of God," where there was a confluence and a desired unity of various faiths and religious beliefs; second, a more immediate commitment to certain shared values that maintained an uncompromising stand on moral principles across religious boundaries. While believing in his grand, long-term goal, Gandhi focused his energies on bridging the many individual divides that contemporary events pushed to the fore.

Gandhi's experience with religions showed him that the refashioning of India's political space demanded a new approach to the problem of religion in general. His critique of theological-political approaches for manifesting nonshared sovereignty led to his desire for a dialogical ethics of a nonviolent way of life that would value the other religion while also allowing for spiritual self-transformation. Gandhi's ventures in the political realm were directed to the same goal of liberative transformation of the public and spiritual selves. Gandhi firmly believed that life was an indivisible whole and that actions and beliefs, whether political or spiritual, were therefore interrelated. He did not think that religious problems could be solely solved by politicians or by enacting laws. Much fundamentalist and religious intolerance arose from a lack of dialogue and mutual understanding among religions, a problem that politicians could not easily solve. For Gandhi, a truly religious person was a caring individual who had to favor "neighborliness" in a multifaith community. This is why he said: "Spiritual experiences are shared by us whether we wish it or not by our lives, not by our speech which is a most imperfect vehicle of experience. Spiritual experiences are deeper even than thought."[45]

The resonances of Gandhi's antifundamentalist thinking, as we have already mentioned, led in many directions. What Gandhi tried to show, in a genuine and practical fashion, was that the ethics of empathy and reciprocity were far more vital for a genuinely shared sovereignty than fundamentalism as a militant principle in opposition to secular state. For him, religion was a work of the ethical, rather than the theological. And he did not draw simple lines between ethics and politics, just as he did not strictly demarcate politics and religion. He was far from being a secular fundamentalist or a religious revivalist, but secularism did not therefore mean for him exclusion of the spiritual from the public sphere. Rather, it meant respect for all men and their spiritual views. Secularism for Gandhi was not the process of banning religious individuals from the public sphere but, on the contrary, created a public realm in which individuals were free to have choice and dialogue with respect to religious creeds. What Gandhi considered was a whole idea of rectification of religious prejudices through a hermeneutic approach to religious scriptures and a public policy of mutual recognition and bestowal of an honorable status on religious doctrines to help individuals liberate themselves from authoritarian forms of religious expression. And here Gandhi becomes an inevitable figure of reference because he puts an end to false choice between "fundamentalism or secularism." He suggests that the political is a relational and dialogical element of the spiritual and sheds a new light on the spiritual as a constitutive factor of the political. It was for such reasons that Muslims like Azad and Ghaffar Khan were inspired by a non-Muslim such as Gandhi. It is worth remembering, as Gandhi repeatedly tells us, that, "No one has a monopoly of truth."[46] We have at most "glimpses" of truth, just as others have their glimpses. In 1947, we find the same idea arising in a response to some Muslims who objected to Gandhi's inclusion of occasional readings of the Qur'an in his prayer meetings. According to Gandhi one had to "remain absolutely faithful to the text [and approach it] with a prayerful and open mind," but he also added that scriptures were "still being corrected."[47] What is fresh and relevant in Gandhi's spiritual pluralism is the alternative it presents both to secularism and to Hindu nationalism as a potential solution to the issues of political plurality and religious diversity in Indian society. Gandhi was conscious that secularism was one of the major instruments for building a democratic Indian polity. He understood the threats that castism, communalism, and religious fundamentalism—all of them carrying risks of separatism and violence—posed to his ideal of a spiritual and pluralistic society. Gandhi's spiritual secularism, unlike that of Nehru, was founded on a commitment to the brotherhood of religious communities and based on their respect for and pursuit of truth. While Gandhi evaluated secularism as a societal or civilizational phenomenon, Jawaharlal Nehru sought to incorporate the outlook at the techno-scientific and administrative levels. Gandhi, however, did not attach any meaning to the term "secular" that would have been beyond Nehru's conception of the Indian state. In September 1946, Gandhi told a Christian missionary: "If I were a dictator, religion and state would be separate. I swear by my religion. I will die for it. But it is my personal affair. The state has nothing to do with it. The state would look after your secular welfare, health, communications, foreign relations, currency and so on, but not your or my religion. That is everybody's personal concern!"[48] This is to say, for Gandhi, secularism was neither another label for Hindu dominance nor a stealthy means of discriminating among Indian citizens. Assuredly, the Hindu ethnonationalists and Muslim fundamentalists were political losers in the debates and infighting during the decade leading up to Indian independence. They both believed that a cohesive ethnocultural group, with a firm religious sense of belonging, could not accept any nationalism other than its own. In 1939, Raja Sahib Mahmudabad, chief lieutenant of the Muslim League's leader, Muhammad Ali Jinnah, wrote to a fellow Muslim: "When we speak of democracy in Islam it is not democracy in the government but in the cultural and social aspects of life. Islam is totalitarian—there is no denying about it. It is the Koran that we should turn to. It is the dictatorship of the Koranic laws that we want—and that we will have—but not through non-violence and Gandhian truth."[49] It is true that when we read such statements, shrewd ethnocentrism might appear more politically powerful than pluralistic tolerance. But there should be no confusion about Gandhi's relevance and power in the context of a rigid and Manichean world. He would speak out unequivocally on how such nationalist or religious sectarianisms would be unjustified and must be opposed. "And yet," as Nehru said, "he was no dreamer living in some fantasy of his own creation, cut off from life and its problems."[50]

CHAPTER SIX

Gandhi and Beyond

The spirit of Gandhi is much stronger today than some people believe.

MARTIN LUTHER KING, JR.

The statement above is as true today as it was when Indian radio broadcast it during Martin Luther King, Jr.'s visit to India in March 1959. And few people exemplified the importance of Gandhi's legacy as clearly as King himself. Along with the South African struggle against apartheid, briefly discussed below, the civil rights campaign led by King is one of the great achievements of nonviolent protest in the decades after Gandhi's death.

King traveled to India in 1959 in search of the roots of the nonviolent social movement that led to Indian independence, studying Mahatma Gandhi's ideals and meeting his followers around the country. On King's return to the United States, the civil rights movement helped transform American race relations, drawing on Gandhi's philosophy as it did so. In King's view, Gandhi was the first thinker-reformer in modern history to reinvent the Christian ethic of love as an instrument for social and collective transformation. The success of the Gandhian strategies that King adopted made him, ultimately, the moral leader of his country and led to one of the most famous nonviolent struggles of modern times. Often labeled the "American Gandhi," Dr. Martin Luther King recognized early on how effective Mahatma Gandhi's nonviolent strategies could be in his own campaigns for integration and voting rights. King not only traveled to India, but also carefully read Gandhi's writings. He became perhaps Gandhi's greatest disciple by embracing *satyagraha* as a means for achieving the emancipation of blacks in America. King was of course influenced by a variety of authors, including Walter Rauschenbusch, George Davis, L. Harold De Wolf, Reinhold Niebuhr, and Paul Tillich, but above all he shaped his strategies along Gandhian lines. In doing so, he indirectly responded to the visionary message of Gandhi who affirmed that, "It may be through the Negroes that the unadulterated message of nonviolence will be delivered to the world."[1]

Confronting America's racial dilemmas, King saw Gandhian philosophy as a new and powerful weapon against injustice. Assessing the importance of the struggle in Montgomery, Alabama, he asserted: "We had hoped to see demonstrated a method that would enable us to continue our struggle while coping with the violence it aroused. Now we see the answer: face violence if necessary, but refuse to return violence. If we respect those who oppose us, they may achieve a new understanding of the human relations involved."[2] King's "personalist" principle of respect for the inherent moral worth of every individual deeply influenced his analysis of human relations and of the complexity of human collectivities. King described personalism as "the theory that the clue to the meaning of ultimate reality is found in personality."[3] King came to regard nonviolence as a natural extension of the organizing principle of "personality." One just has to look at King's innumerable references to the idea of "personal God" and to "the sacredness of human personality" to understand the theoretical and practical connections between nonviolence and personalism in King's thoughts and actions. He explained this influence, thus: "in recent months I have also become more and more convinced of the reality of a personal God. True, I have always believed in the personality of God. But in the past years the idea of a personal God was little more than a metaphysical category, which I found theologically and philosophically satisfying. Now it is a living reality that has been validated in the experience of everyday life. . . . To say God is personal is not to make him an object among others or attribute to him the finiteness and limitations human personality; it is to take what is finest and noblest in our consciousness and affirm its perfect existence in him."[4] In one form or another, King's testimony to personalism and his ideas about the dignity of human personality provided him with a metaphysical grounding for his understanding of human goodness and his break with orthodox theology and dogmatic religion. The notion that human beings are essentially good and formed in the image of

God was compelling and provocative to King and helped prepare his intellectual odyssey to nonviolence.

King's ultimate optimism about human nature was founded on three points. First, he held that the validity of nonviolence arose from the Christian concept of "agape" as the only moral absolute. Second, he believed in the redemptive possibility of nonviolence in human history and thought that moral progress showed the universe was on the side of justice. Finally, King believed that nonviolent resistance to evil and injustice would produce reconciliation and what he called the "Beloved Community." In the final analysis, King considered nonviolence not only a method for persuading the opponent about specific matters, but also as strategy for achieving deep social and political change. His use of nonviolence as a solidaristic approach to human co-existence appears as the organizing principle of all his thought and actions. He came to understand the nonviolent struggle for social justice as the immanence of God in history. The commitment to justice and to struggle against evil was, in King's view, a spiritual act and a moral duty. Like Gandhi, King believed in a community of greater love and justice that was supposed to fulfill God's will. In many of King's speeches and sermons, he proclaimed that the struggle for justice not only reveals God's purpose but is made possible by God's will to actualize it. He also saw "the love of God operating in the human heart"[5] as a community-creating force. In other words, King thought of justice as a worldly term and expected the Beloved Community to be achieved within history. King illustrated what he meant by the Beloved Community when he wrote: "But we must remember when we boycott that a boycott is not an end within itself; it is merely a means to awaken a sense of shame within the oppressor and challenge his false sense of superiority. But the end is reconciliation; the end is redemption; the end is the creation of the beloved community."[6] King did not perceive love as an abstract principle. For him, love was the principle of social solidarity, expressing itself through a practical concern for human personality and constant respect for the common good. In this respect, King believed that the church had failed in its mission to promote the love exemplified by Jesus, while, ironically, the Gandhian principle of nonviolence had helped to restore the power of Christian love. According to King, "Gandhi was probably the first person in history to lift the love ethic of Jesus above mere interaction between individuals to a powerful and effective social force on a large scale. Love for Gandhi was a potent instrument for social and collective transformation. It was in this Gandhian emphasis on love and nonviolence that I discovered the method for social reform that I had been seeking for so many months."[7] What impressed King about the Gandhian idea of love was its concern for a worldwide fellowship that lifted neighborly concern beyond one's race, class, nation, and religion. As such, Gandhi conceived the whole *satyagraha* movement as an effort to transform the paradigm of hatred into that of love. Indeed what Gandhi stressed was not only the absence of hatred but the presence of neighborly love: "Non-cooperation without love is satanic; noncooperation with love is godly . . . our non-cooperation also springs from love. Without it, everything is hollow. Love is not merely the master key, it is the only key."[8] For Gandhi as for King, love for human beings went hand in hand with love for God. Gandhi developed this idea in the course of a speech in Lausanne on December 8, 1931: "Love for God is not to be distinct from love for man. But if there was a conflict between the two loves, I would know there was a conflict in the man himself. I should therefore invite him to carry on the search within himself. But when you find love for man divorced from love for God, you will find at basis a base motive. Real love for man I regard to be utterly impossible without love for God."[9] Gandhi, here again, stressed the importance of love as a cohesive force that can transform the individual and the community. To Gandhi, it is a power that enables humanity to move toward the recognition of human dignity and the universal realization of justice. Though King connected his concept of "agape" to the love ethic of Christ, his formulation of love as a neighborly emotion and a communitarian sentiment was closely related to the Gandhian definition of love as a foundation of all human relationship and of all human intercourse, whether social, economic, or political. King related the centrality of love to political resistance and to the development of community. Ultimately, he would use the Gandhian concept of "neighborliness" for his vision of a just and reconciled society.

Martin Luther King's contribution to reconciliation in

American society and in the world at large is widely recognized. His vision of a reconciled society was that of an inclusive community with a sense of responsibility. King explained: "At the heart of all that civilization has meant and developed is 'community'—the mutually cooperative and voluntary venture of man to assume a semblance of responsibility for his brother."[10] King's conception of "reconciliation" is best described as total connectedness, as a network of reciprocity. The recognition of one's indebtedness and one's responsibility to others leads in King's philosophy to an awareness of the interdependent character of life. "In a real sense," said King, "all life is interrelated. The agony of the poor impoverishes the rich; the betterment of the poor enriches the rich. We are inevitably our brother's keeper because we are our brother's brother. Whatever affects one directly affects all indirectly."[11] King's conception of a reconciled society does not appear to have room for an individual good that may be opposed to the common good. In other words, the self can never truly separate itself from others within the community. Mutual recognition and reconciliation embody not only a sense of inclusiveness, but also mutual dependence. It is interesting to note that King's notion of inclusiveness is an intercultural imperative and does not rely on a monocultural sense of belonging. King proclaimed: "All men are interdependent. Every nation is an heir of a vast treasure of ideas and labor to which both the living and the dead of all nations have contributed. . . . We are everlasting debtors to known and unknown men and women."[12] King's vision of the Beloved

Community thus brings together the two themes of emancipation and self-transformation. While much of Gandhi's teachings and writings were based on self-sacrifice and nonpossession as means to attain a universal harmony among human communities, King insisted on the "world-wide brotherhood" and an ability "to remain vigilant to face the challenge of change." According to Gandhi, "Those who have followed out this vow of voluntary poverty to the fullest extent possible . . . testify that when you dispossess yourself of everything you have, you really possess all the treasures of the world."[13] King would passionately bring the Gandhian principle of moral and spiritual self-transformation into conversation with the challenges of the global world by affirming: "The large house in which we live demands that we transform this world-wide neighborhood into a world-wide brotherhood. Together we must learn to live as brothers or together we will be forced to perish as fools. . . . We must work passionately and indefatigably to bridge the gulf between our scientific progress and our moral progress. One of the great problems of mankind is that we suffer from a poverty of the spirit which stands in glaring contrast to our scientific and technological abundance. The richer we have become materially, the poorer we have become morally and spiritually."[14] As we can see, King's vision of reconciliation and interrelatedness evolves into a global intercultural imperative. Both Gandhi and King present us with attractive proposals for applying the two concepts of "emancipation" and "reconciliation" to postmodern times. Ultimately, for both of them, the path toward

emancipation and reconciliation in a connected world must ⌄
embrace the radicality of "fellowship" and "neighborliness" as
the window between cultures that makes reconciliation possible. By taking Gandhi beyond India, King hoped to achieve a
fundamental change in the structures of American society, not
just to improve relations between races. King saw the African-
American nonviolent movement as an effort to revive the
perennial dream of American democracy and tried to bring a
fresh meaning to it by formulating his own dream as that of
equal opportunity and solidarity. King pronounced:

> This will be the day when we shall bring into full real-
> ization the American dream—a dream yet unfulfilled.
> A dream of equality of opportunity, of privilege and
> property widely distributed; a dream of a land where
> men will not take necessities from the many to give
> luxuries to the few, a dream of a land where men will
> not argue that the color of a man's skin determined the
> content of his character; a dream of a nation where all
> our gifts and resources are held not for ourselves alone
> but as instruments of service for the rest of humanity;
> the dream of a country where every man will respect
> the dignity and worth of human personality—that is
> the dream. . . . Whenever it is fulfilled, we will emerge
> from the bleak and desolate midnight of man's inhu-
> manity to man into the bright and glowing daybreak of
> freedom and justice for all of God's children.[15]

King extended his vision for America into a vision of a world in which all people can share in the wealth of the earth and where peace with justice will prevail over war and military conflict. King's conception of global emancipation was based on the idea that individuals are not morally isolated, but find their ethical meaning in relation with others. Structural changes, he thought, become a global possibility once individuals find their meaning as actors of interconnectivity rather than acting out and reacting against ignorance, intolerance, and hatred.

It goes without saying that the new society of King's imagination cannot come about without intense suffering; a suffering not just imposed by external forces, but one voluntarily undergone to transform the self and the others. There is obviously a relationship in King's thought and action between nonviolent resistance to evil and injustice and suffering without retaliation. This is what King meant when he affirmed: "Recognizing the necessity for suffering I have tried to make of it a virtue."[16] King, like Gandhi, considered suffering as a redemptive act for both the black community and the white community in America. It was also an essential ingredient of his vision of the reconciled society. That is to say, King's model of the Beloved Community, like Gandhi's idea of *Rama Rajya*, is intrinsically moral, a place where suffering is not an excuse for violence, but a challenge to be morally overcome. King perceived the "beloved," "reconciled," or "integrated" community as the definite expression of moral principles of social solidarity and mutual love. The quest for emancipation and reconciliation meant for him adopting a vision of human interaction that flowed from a sense of mutual understanding and the possibility of forgiveness for causing suffering. Ultimately the salvific meaning of King's and Gandhi's nonviolent action is mutual love and solidarity. Both envisioned fundamental changes in political, social, and economic affairs, and both insisted that the pursuit of new paradigms for emancipation and reconciliation should be constrained by an ethical outlook. One can make a reasonable claim that the journeys of Gandhi and King were primarily ethical or, more accurately, spiritual journeys in the company of ethics. There was a moral wisdom in their search for nonviolence, wisdom that translated their metaphysical and spiritual beliefs into ethical principles to guide their agendas. King's and Gandhi's moral imperative remained grounded not only in the state of "being" nonviolent but in the act of "becoming" nonviolent, of embracing what I have called here the Gandhian moment. For both Gandhi and King, nonviolence meets the requirements of ethics. Hence, King's famous Dream Speech at the Lincoln Memorial, where he called out with confidence: "Let us not seek to satisfy our thirst for freedom by drinking from the cup of bitterness and hatred. We must forever conduct our struggle on the high plane of dignity and discipline. We must not allow our creative protest to degenerate into physical violence. Again and again we must rise to the majestic heights of meeting physical force with soul force."[17] Gandhi and King both formulated the notion of transformative liberation as a "freedom to become" rather than simply as "freedom from oppression." They believed there had to be a moral agency and moral coloring to one's effort to become free. Gandhi and King would further propose that constructing an ethically coherent community of reconciliation asks for a high correlation between the political praxis of a community and its moral responsibility. Structural change in a pluralistic and conflictual world must be pursued with an enlightened and rigorously ethical understanding of individual responsibility and responsible freedom. One of the pragmatic advantages of the universal acceptance of nonviolence that King and Gandhi advocated is that substantial power is gained from ethical consistency within the movement. For example, in the case of King's nonviolent movement, there was a practical advantage to black Americans being viewed as ethically consistent, since the goals of the movement were partially pursued by convincing opponents that it was the right and ethical choice to grant civil rights to black Americans. Ethical consistency helped convince racist Americans that black Americans possessed the political ability to join the empowered population and countered the old perception that they were subhuman and politically disorganized.

King and Gandhi believed, and in their actions showed, that morality crosses boundaries. Though King believed that the acceptance of black civil rights had to be reached as a personal ethical decision, this did not stop him from strongly believing that his moral intuitions were universal. King avoided drawing lines between black and white (as did Gandhi essentially between Indians and British), but instead framed the civil rights movement as an ethical struggle for all Americans, regardless of race. Consider these excerpts from his 1963 speech at the Lincoln Memorial:

> When the architects of our republic wrote the magnificent words of the Constitution and the Declaration of Independence, they were signing a promissory note to which every American was to fall heir. This note was a promise that all men, yes, black men as well as white men, would be guaranteed the 'unalienable Rights' of 'Life, Liberty and the pursuit of Happiness.' It is obvious today that America has defaulted on this promissory note, insofar as her citizens of color are concerned. Instead of honoring this sacred obligation, America has given the Negro people a bad check, a check which has come back marked 'insufficient funds.' . . . The marvelous new militancy which has engulfed the Negro community must not lead us to a distrust of all white people, for many of our white brothers, as evidenced by their presence here today, have come to realize that their destiny is tied up with our destiny. And they have come to realize that their freedom is inextricably bound to our freedom.[18]

King's motivation for nonviolence was primarily deontological, drawing from his spiritual convictions. He did not see the pursuit of nonviolent action as a zero-sum game in which black Americans would pursue their goals at the expense of white Americans, but as an associative and ethically righteous project, which inherently demanded the participation of all. Nonviolence was an all-inclusive principle to King, as it was to Gandhi. The quests for liberation for Indians in India and for equal rights for blacks in America were indirectly quests for justice for others who suffered injustice and oppression. With his prophetic proclamation that "injustice anywhere is a threat to justice everywhere," King was able to appeal to the idea of a universal dream beyond the American Dream. King's universal dream not only revived Gandhi's vision of nonviolence as a global project, but it also broadened it. King, like Gandhi, was confident that if those who were committed to nonviolence would continue to practice it, they would bring nations closer in order for humans to live together with respect and dignity. To commit to nonviolence was to do more than merely restrain oneself physically. It was to commit to an ethical course of conduct, a way of life, and ultimately a spiritual attitude both for individual and community alike. Acting nonviolently is *ipso facto* to respect the other. It is a principle that has its roots in mutuality, as Gandhi explained: "the end of nonviolent war is always an agreement, never dictation, much less humiliation of the opponent."[19]

In seeking to bring the world closer together, to forge bonds through certain universal commitments, neither Gandhi nor King sought to erase cultural differences. For them, the search for a nonviolent democracy was also a quest for a plural world, not in spite of our differences and divergences but thanks to our differences and divergences. As pluralists, Gandhi and King realized that there is no such thing as a single homogeneous religious or cultural community. They were convinced that the future of our global civilization depends on our ability to live together with our diversities, if not in harmony, at least with a capacity of dialogue and mutual understanding. They were both willing to admit that at the bottom of their hope for a better future, based on a shared vision of solidarity and reconciliation, lay a metaphysical and spiritual vision of a gathering of persons in a global community. King and Gandhi were confident that nonviolence could progress through human effort and God's help. King explained this hope in a passage of his book *Strength to Love:*

> Although man's moral pilgrimage may never reach a destination point on earth, his never-ceasing strivings may bring him ever closer to the city of righteousness. And though the Kingdom of god may remain not yet as universal reality in history, in the present it may exist in such isolated forms as in judgment, in personal devotion, and in some group life. . . . Above all, we must be reminded anew that God is at work in his universe. He is not outside the world looking on within a sort of cold indifference. . . . As we struggle to defeat the forces of evil, the God of the universe struggles

with us. Evil dies on the seashore, not merely because of man's endless struggle against it, but because of God's power to defeat it.[20]

Behind King's conception lay his assumption of what he called, "The solidarity of the human family," meaning recognition of one's indebtedness to other persons, communities, and cultures. That is, King was not concerned about justice for blacks as opposed to justice for whites; he was concerned about justice for everyone around the world. "Let us be dissatisfied," he wrote, "until rat-infested, vermin-filled slums will be a thing of a dark past and every family will have a decent sanitary house in which to live. Let us be dissatisfied until the empty stomachs of Mississippi are filled and the idle industries of Appalachia are revitalized. . . . Let us be dissatisfied until our brothers of the Third World of Asia, Africa and Latin America will no longer be the victims of imperialist exploitation, but will be lifted from the long night of poverty, illiteracy and disease."[21]

Although King's assassination in 1968 was a massive blow to the nonviolent campaign for civil rights in America, his legacy took American democracy in a new direction. By adopting the Gandhian techniques of nonviolent resistance, King became a leading figure not just in the American but in the world struggle for peace and justice. According to Greg Moses: "King's death marked the end of an era, but in the broader life of the mind a logic of nonviolence was just beginning to make its way into the world."[22] King gave black consciousness around the world a novel sense of solidarity and self-confidence in its struggle against racism and segregation. But he also gave a new life to the Gandhian philosophy of nonviolence. The Gandhian-Kingian legacy played an important role in reviving nonviolent protest around the world for the next four decades under the leadership of global figures such as Nelson Mandela, Desmond Tutu, Dalai Lama, and others. For some of these leaders, nonviolence remained a moral principle and a way of life. For others, it was simply an effective strategy against injustice and as a tactical weapon in the struggle for democracy. It goes without saying that outside India and America, Gandhi and King were widely considered as symbols for struggle against imperialism and racism.

The 1980s witnessed a powerful global nonviolent movement that symbolized growing awareness of alternatives to using war and violence as instruments of policymaking. This awakening reached its climax in South Africa, especially among leaders like Archbishop Desmond Tutu and Nelson Mandela, who were trying to find a way to put an end to South Africa's racist apartheid regime. As Mandela later stated in his moving and exhilarating autobiography entitled *Long Walk to Freedom:* "For me nonviolence was not a moral principle but a strategy; there is no moral goodness in using ineffective weapon."[23] Mandela believed that it was vital in a political struggle to find a balance between violence and nonviolence. "Violence and nonviolence," he asserted, "are not mutually exclusive; it is the predominance of the one or the other that labels a struggle."[24] Actually, Mandela, like King and Gandhi, understood that erasing hatred of the opponent and living harmoniously with the other were the best ways to ensure good governance. As he wrote after his negotiations with W. F. de Klerk: "To make peace with an enemy, one must work with the enemy, and that enemy becomes your partner."[25] It is, however, true that, unlike Gandhi and King, Mandela was not drawn to nonviolence by the way of faith. But he drew his inspiration directly from the Gandhian tradition of nonviolent activism in pursuit of a politics informed by truth. His nonviolence, like that of King and Gandhi, was not passive, a mere politics of restraint, but active and entailed the pursuit of meaningful dialogue and exchange with opponents. Mandela was in every respect a figure of immense moral stature, and it was his great achievement that South African blacks moved toward black rule without satisfying their desire of revenge against the whites.

Mandela did not, of course, work alone. Perhaps his most prominent ally in the nonviolent transition of South Africa to democracy was Archbishop Desmond Tutu. Few people today think about Tutu outside the context of the struggle against apartheid. But he should also be considered as a pivotal theologian of emancipation and reconciliation. Tutu's conception of *"ubuntu* theology," with its great vision of community-building and nonviolent action, is a tremendous achievement with enormous potential to foster fellowship. In the same manner as Gandhi and King, Tutu incorporated an understanding of social empathy and political reconciliation in his vision of God as a source of redemption and hope. Tutu's distinctive understanding of human relationships can be described by his use of the Bantu concept of *ubuntu*, which means "humanity" and derives from a classical Xhosa expression: "*ubuntu ungamntu ngabanye abantu*" (each individual's humanity is ideally expressed in relationship with others).[26] Tutu's idea of human relationships is rooted in what we can call his "spirituality of fellowship," practiced as a politics of belonging, participating, and sharing. As he observes: "According to *ubuntu*, it is not a greater good to be successful through being aggressively competitive and successful for the expense of others. In the end, our purpose is social and communal harmony as well being. *Ubuntu* does not say, 'I think, therefore I am.' It says rather: 'I am because I belong. I participate. I share.' Harmony, friendliness, community are great goods. Social harmony is for us the *summum bonum*, the greatest good. Anything that subverts, that undermines this sought-after good is to be avoided like the plague. Anger, resentment, lust for revenge, even success through aggressive competitiveness, are corrosive of this good."[27] Tutu's spirituality of fellowship echoed Gandhi's communitarian ethos of interfaith dialogue and communal harmony. Tutu accepted the Gandhian-Kingian concept of "love" as a means for spiritual and material transformation of the individual and the community. As a theologian of solidarity and reconciliation, Tutu sought to provide us with the spiritual resources to further explore the idea of community as a forum of differences and otherness. For Tutu, the struggle to dismantle the apartheid regime was not least an effort to create a new community of fellowship and solidarity. He was not seeking simply to abolish the institutions of racism and apartheid, but to change people's perceptions of themselves and to restructure justice and peace in South Africa. He wrote: "The evil of apartheid is perhaps not so much the untold misery and anguish it has caused its victims (great and traumatic as these must be), no, its pernicious nature, indeed its blasphemous character is revealed in its effect on God's children when it makes them doubt that they are God's children."[28] Like Mandela and unlike King, Tutu was not an absolute Gandhian about nonviolence. Still, despite their moments of doubt about the effectiveness of Gandhian nonviolent action, Mandela and Tutu shared a vision of communitarian reconciliation that recognized the importance of Gandhian and Kingian philosophies of nonviolence as a way of rethinking the relationship between power and people in an increasingly interconnected world.

Political and social action without violence has always been overshadowed by violence in the news and media and thus in our collective memory. But we should recall that nonviolent struggles for peace, freedom, and democracy have been pivotal in many of the great nation-changing popular movements of the past hundred years: in various campaigns against colonial rule, against communist rule in Poland and elsewhere behind the Iron Curtain, and against apartheid in South Africa. The greatest misconception about political struggle and nation-building is that violence is always the key to defeating injustice and fighting a dictatorship. But during the past century, Mahatma Gandhi, Martin Luther King Jr., Nelson Mandela, Desmond Tutu, Dalai Lama, and many others have proven the power of nonviolence. And there are less famous, but no less impressive cases, such as that of the Danes who steadfastly refused to comply with the laws of their Nazi occupiers during World War II and that of the Argentinean mothers who helped to topple military rule with their peaceful protests against the murders of their children by the secret police. All show how oppressive rulers can be defied not by the force of arms, but by the force of soul. As Gene Sharp puts it, "nonviolent action is possible, and is capable of wielding great power even against ruthless rulers and military regimes, because it attacks the most vulnerable characteristic of all hierarchical institutions and governments: dependence on the governed."[29]

The Gandhian moment begins in the hearts and minds of individuals reorienting their relationship with the state and opening themselves to the possibilities of nonviolence and deep engagement with others. Writ large, it can inspire extraordinary political and social change. The Indian independence movement mobilized millions who were prepared to suffer imprisonment, beating, humiliation, and death in order to defy the British Raj. India gained its independence by developing and nurturing conscientiously Gandhian values. But commitment to Gandhian ideals can be fragile. Gandhi did not live long enough to see the abandonment of his ideals and methods by Indian political elites and economic decision-makers as they built the new Indian republic. With the exception of Vinoba Bhave, Jayaprakash Narayan, and few others who followed the Gandhian notion that society must control the state and not vice versa, the Gandhian model of nonviolent civil resistance and democratization of political power found its true voices outside India. No doubt not all nonviolent movements are successful or endure after they have achieved success. But neither are all violent revolutions successful. In the past decades since Gandhi's assassination we have seen many insurrections overthrow unjust regimes—in Africa, in Asia, in the Middle East, and elsewhere—only to see the same injustices come back with different faces. The fact that Gandhian approaches do not always work does not imply that there are better methods. Nor should we assume that Gandhi's sole achievement was to lay out strategies to achieve specific political goals. We need to look at Gandhi's legacy not only as a political strategy for civil resistance, but as a broader emancipatory praxis that is creative and constructive under what me might call normal political conditions. There is no reason to think that Gandhi's ideas cannot be globalized—that they cannot be so extended as to curb violence on a much grander scale. The key, though, remains the Gandhian moment of individual reinvention.

....

CHAPTER SEVEN

Conclusion

GANDHI TODAY

The past two years will remain momentous in the history of Gandhian nonviolence for people in the Middle East and around the world. Despite their geographic and cultural diversity, nonviolent movements in Egypt, Tunisia, Syria, Bahrain, and Yemen exhibited a remarkable similarity to Gandhi's and King's campaigns for checking power and opposing violence in India and in the United States decades ago. Never before have people in the region mobilized in such vast numbers to shake off the chains of their autocratic regimes. This raises the hopeful prospect that nonviolent campaigns for democracy might be the essential paradigm of change in the Middle East and Maghreb—areas of the world that have been marked by violence for so long. Many in the West are familiar with the nonviolent strategies that helped bring civil rights to the United States as well as democracy to Eastern Europe. But this path has been discounted in the Muslim world where the media has perpetuated stereotypes of Muslims as dangerous and violent fanatics. The blood that has been shed in some countries since the first heady days of the Arab Spring may give fuel to these crude ideas, and it would be naïve to herald the dawn of a new Gandhian age. But it should no longer be possible to cling to the old idea that Arab, Turkish, and Iranian populations are uninterested in seeking democratic freedoms or capable of liberating themselves nonviolently from their authoritarian rulers. Millions of Egyptians, Tunisians, Iranians, Yemenites, Syrians, and others have proved their accusers wrong by mobilizing against their authoritarian rulers and seeking to do so without violence. These movements should remind the world that many nonviolent Muslim activists and thinkers have played a role in opposing and checking the levels of violence both within their own communities and against others. The nonviolent campaigns erupting across dominantly Islamic countries today, largely based among the young middle class, clearly indicate a growing ethical commitment to norms of transparency, negotiation, compromise, and mutual respect. Their links to the networks of global civil society, tied together by information technologies from Facebook to YouTube, reinforce a universal ethic, as Gandhi preached, which transcends religious and cultural particularities, even as it is channeled through local grassroots movements. This is where Gandhi's spiritual approach to politics comes into its own and distinguishes itself from fundamentalist approaches to religion, which divide people who need to work together. Far from being utopian, the Gandhian emphasis on an ethical politics based on nonviolence and mutual respect may be the most practical path to achieve democracy in a region exhausted from the seemingly endless repression and bloodshed that has arisen from the belief that violence is the real source of power. What we saw in Tunisia, and on many occasions on the streets of Cairo and Tehran, suggests that Gandhi understood power better than the autocrats and ayatollahs who are now trying to hang on. "Even the most despotic government cannot stand except for the consent of the governed, which consent is often forcibly procured by the despot," Gandhi wrote. "Immediately the subject ceases to fear the despotic force, his power is gone."[1]

One such government that now faces dissent from the governed is Iran's. There is already an evident similarity between the civil disobedience movement in today's Iran and successful nonviolent movements led by Gandhi in South Africa and in India. What is most important in Iran is that the massive outpouring of antifundamentalist sentiments there is so far doubtlessly nonviolent and peaceful. Chief among the slogans of the demonstrators has been the condemnation of violence. Iranian society is in the midst of an epoch-making renaissance in its political culture and discourse. This transformation in political values, norms, symbols, and everyday codes of behavior is most evident in the peaceful and nonviolent action of all those who have been protesting against theocratic rule and pure exercise of power without ethics in Iran.

Many young Iranians in the past few years have marched silently and lit candles. Others have worn green wristbands or ribbons and carried flowers. Gandhi chose a spinning wheel as a symbol of his idea of nonviolence. A spinning wheel represented two different messages: the main symbol to protest against an unethical idea of civilization; and a symbol of resistance to the British-made clothes that had replaced the Indian handmade clothes. Today, the true hero of the Iranian civic movement is the emerging republican model of nonviolent resistance and ethical politics that provide the clearest guideline and vision for Iran's gradual transition to an open society. Post-revolutionary Iran has experienced the failure of two major political paradigms in the last thirty years: revolutionary leftism and ideological Islam. They each failed in practice as well as in theory, and the Iranian people no longer trust the groups associated with them. It is evident that nonviolent action is the new paradigm that is attempting to define itself distinctly and overcome the intellectual and political weaknesses of its predecessors.

There is common agreement among demonstrators and civil activists that the main divide in contemporary Iran is between authoritarian violence and democratic nonviolence. Though this nonviolent paradigm is still in the making, it can nonetheless be characterized as a Gandhian moment in Iran or, more accurately, as the manifestation of many individual Gandhian moments. The protest movement in Iran remains nonviolent and civil in its methods of creating social change while also seeking an ethical dimension to Iranian politics. This implies that Iranian civil society is ready to make a distinction between two approaches: searching for truth and solidarity versus lying and using violence. The Gandhian moment in Iran exemplifies the possibility of creating a politics of living responsibly and putting ethics ahead of power relations. Basically, Iran's public discourse has changed as citizens have drunk deeply from the well of nonviolence. Today, young Iranians couch their conversations about politics in a moral vocabulary. For every mention of rights, they mention responsibility. Iranians need not read *Hind Swaraj* to live responsibly, but reading *Hind Swaraj* can help.

Regardless of how things ultimately turn out in Iran, the protests against religious authoritarianism have provided us with yet another example of Gandhi's influence in democratizing modernity. What protests in Iran show us is that if we are in an era where politics are becoming a site for higher responsibilities and concern for others, we must recognize that the Gandhian moment of politics is not merely "the other possibility" for our world, but "the possibility realized in the first instance."

Gandhi believed that human destiny is to move toward nonviolence. It is true that new forms of conflict and violations of human rights around the world render this a problematic view. The recent war in Iraq showed us that commitment to nonviolence is not yet so widespread that it can reliably stop the dominating will of one nation or of one man. However, it is also true that there is a growing awareness of the need to get beyond violence. To move even further requires renewed commitment to education in Gandhian ideals, to replacing the notions of "fundamentalism" and "nationalism" with that of nonviolence. Over time we can hope that a change in the guiding principles of individual morality can lead to a basic change in the principles that guide the life of nations. We just need to remember what Gandhi said: "I can only say that my own experience in organizing nonviolent action for a half of a century fills me with hope for the future."[2]

Notes

ONE *Introduction*

1. Hannah Arendt, *Between Past and Future* (New York: Meridian Books, 1965), 149.

2. In *Young India*, March 1930. As quoted in Raghavan N. Iyer, *The Moral and Political Thought of Mahatma Gandhi* (Delhi: Oxford University Press, 1973), 278.

3. Mohandas K. Gandhi, *Hind Swaraj and Other Writings*, Anthony J. Parel, ed. (Cambridge: Cambridge University Press, 1997), 98.

4. Quoted by J. V. Naik, "Relevance of Gandhi" in S. N. Datye, *Rethinking Mahatma Gandhi: Relevance of Gandhian Thought and Leadership in the 21st Century* (Delhi: Kalinga Publications, 2001), 13.

5. Rajmohan Gandhi, *Mohandas: A True Story of a Man, His People and an Empire* (New Delhi: Penguin Books, 2006), 196.

6. Judith M. Brown, *Gandhi: Prisoner of Hope* (New Haven: Yale University Press, 1989), 394.

7. Quoted in Thomas Merton, ed., *Gandhi on Non-Violence* (New York: New Directions, 1965), 74.

8. *Young India* (April 14, 1929).

9. Mohandas K. Gandhi, *Towards Everlasting Peace*, A. T. Hingorani, ed. (Bombay: Bharatiya Vidya Bhavan, 1956), 217.

10. Mohandas K. Gandhi, *Ethical Religion* (Madras: S. Ganesan, 1922), 8–11.

11. *Harijan* (April 20, 1935).

12. *Young India* (March 1925).

13. Quoted in Thomas Pantham, "Thinking with Mahatma: Beyond Liberal Democracy," *Political Theory* 11, no. 2 (May 1983), 180.

14. Joan V. Bondurant, *Conquest of Violence: The Gandhian Philosophy of Conflict*, rev. ed. (Los Angeles: University of California Press, 1965), 3–4.

TWO   *Principles of Gandhian Politics*

1. *Harijan* (May 27, 1939), 139.

2. Ibid. (September 24, 1938), 269

3. Raghavan N. Iyer, *The Moral and Political Thought of Mahatma Gandhi* (London: Grover Press, 1983, tome 3), 12.

4. *Young India* (Navajivan, Ahmedabad: April 10, 1924, 1981), 122.

5. Ibid. (March 24, 1920), 4.

6. David Hardiman, *Gandhi: In His Time and Ours* (Delhi: Permanent Black, 2003), 21.

7. Quoted in Gopinath Dhawan, *The Political Philosophy of Mahatma Gandhi* (Delhi: The Gandhi Peace Foundation, 1990), 243.

8. M. K. Gandhi, *Hind Swaraj and Other Writings* (Cambridge: Cambridge University Press, 1997), 92.

9. *Young India* (August 6, 1931), 203.

10. Ibid. (December 1, 1927), 104.

11. M. K. Gandhi, *From Yeravda Mandir* (Navajivan, Ahmedabad: 1945), 46.

12. *Young India* (Navajivan, Ahmedabad: January 8, 1925, 1981).

13. *Harijan*, July 6, 1947, quoted in M. P. Mathai, *Mahatma Gandhi's World-View* (New Delhi: Gandhi Peace Foundation, 2000), 144.

14. *Young India* (July 2, 1932), 162.

15. *Harijan* (July 26, 1942), 238.

16. *Young India*, December 1924, quoted in Ramashray Roy, *Self and Society: A Study in Gandhian Thought* (New Delhi; Beverly Hills: Sage Publications in collaboration with United Nations University, Tokyo, 1984, c1985), 167.

17. *Young India* (November 1, 1928).

18. M. K. Gandhi, *Collected Works of Mahatma Gandhi* 35: 294.

19. M. K. Gandhi, *CWMG* 26: 52.

20. *Harijan* (January 30, 1937).

21. M. K. Gandhi, *CWMG* 21: 246.

22. Bhikhu Parekh, *Colonialism, Tradition and Reform: An Analysis of Gandhi's Political Discourse* (London: Sage Publications, 1989), 71–72.

23. M. K. Gandhi, Letter dated June 1, 1942, quoted in Nirmal Kumar Bose, *Selections from Gandhi* (Ahmedabad: Navajivan Publishing House, 1950), 7.

24. M. K. Gandhi, *Young India*, October 9, 1931, quoted by N. Radhakrishnan, "The Gandhian Alternatives and the Challenges of the New Millennium" in *International Workshop on Nonviolence in the Twentieth Century and Their Lessons for the Twenty First October 5–12, 1999, New Delhi, 1999*.

25. M. K. Gandhi, *Young India*, (January 6, 1921).

26. M. K. Gandhi, *CWMG*, 7: 338.

27. Quoted in, M. K. Gandhi, *All Men Are Brothers*, Krishna Kripalani, ed. (Paris: UNESCO, 1969), 62.

28. *Young India* (October 23, 1924).

29. *Harijan* (March 21, 1934).

30. Quoted in D. G. Tendulkar, *Mahatma: Life of Mohandas Karamchand Gandhi*, vol. 7 October 1946 (Bombay: Vithalbhai K. Jhaveri, 1953), 264.

31. *Harijan* (February 10, 1940).

32. Quoted in Anand T. Hingorani, ed., *The Supreme Power* (Bombay: Pearl Publications, 1963), 57.

33. *Young India* (December 1924).

34. *Sarvodaya* (January 1939), quoted in Raghavan N. Iyer, ed., *The Moral and Political Writings of Mahatma Gandhi*, vol. 2, (Oxford: The Clarendon Press, 1987), 602.

35. M. K. Gandhi, *The Essential Writings of Mahatma Gandhi*, by Raghavan N. Iyer, ed. (New Delhi, India: Oxford University Press, 2000), 174.

36. *Young India*, December 1, 1920, quoted in Bhikhu Parekh, *Gandhi's Political Philosophy: A Critical Examination* (London: Macmillan Press, 1989), 125.

37. Quoted in Raghavan N. Iyer, *The Moral and Political Writings of Mahatma Gandhi*, vol. 2, 355.

38. *Harijan*, September 1, 1940, quoted in Bhikhu Parekh, *Gandhi's Political Philosophy*, 116.

39. *Harijan* (July 28, 1946).

THREE   *The Critique of Modern Civilization*

1. Quoted in Shrinam Narayan (ed.), *Selected Works of Mahatma Gandhi*, vol. 71 (Ahmedabad: Navijavan Publishing House, 1969), 130.

2. M. K. Gandhi, *Hind Swaraj and Other Writings*, Anthony J. Parel, ed. (Cambridge: Cambridge University Press, 1997), 7.

3. Ibid., *Introduction*, 25.

4. Ibid., 67.

5. Ibid., 53.

6. Ibid., 35–37.

7. Bhikhu Parekh, *Gandhi's Political Philosophy*, 35.

8. M. K. Gandhi, *CWMG*, 32: 219.

9. M. K. Gandhi, *CWMG*, 10: 36–38.

10. *Young India* (August 11, 1927).

11. Quoted in Bhikhu Parekh, *Colonialism, Tradition and Reform: An Analysis of Gandhi's Political Discourse* (New Delhi: Sage Publications, 1989), 215–216.

12. M. K. Gandhi, *Hind Swaraj and Other Writings*, Anthony J. Parel, ed. (Cambridge: Cambridge University Press, 1997), 52.

13. M. K. Gandhi, "Speech at Buddha Birth Anniversary," May 9, 1925, quoted in *CWMG* 27: 61–62.

14. M. K. Gandhi, "Speech at Meeting in Lausanne," December 8, 1931, quoted in Raghavan N. Iyer, ed., *The Moral and Political Writings of Mahatma Gandhi*, vol. 2 (Oxford: Clarendon Press, 1986), 164.

15. *Young India* (July 2, 1931).

16. *Harijan* (July 28, 1946).

17. Quoted in B. N. Ganguli, *Gandhi's Social Philosophy: Perspective and Relevance* (New Delhi: Council for Social Development, 1973), 145.

18. *Young India* (May 6, 1931).

FOUR *Gandhi's Public Philosophy*

1. M. K. Gandhi, "Enlightened Anarchy—A Political Ideal," *Sarvodaya*, 1–39, in Richard L. Johnson, *Gandhi's Experiments with Truth* (Oxford: Lexington Books, 2006), 134.

2. Mahatma Gandhi, *Selected Political Writings*, Dennis Dalton, ed. (Indianapolis: Hackett Publishing Company, 1996), 49.

3. M. K. Gandhi, *Non-violence in Peace and War*, vol. 2, Bharatan Kumarappa, ed. (Ahmedabad: 1949), 269.

4. Srinivas Murthy, *Mahatma Gandhi and Leo Tolstoy Letters* (Long Beach: Long Beach Publications, 1987), 13.

5. M. K. Gandhi, *Hind Swaraj or Indian Home Rule* (Gujarat, Ahmedabad: Navajivan Publishing House, 1938).

6. M. K. Gandhi, *CWMG*, 51 (New Delhi: Publications Division, 1999), 220.

7. M. K. Gandhi, in *Harijan*, November 5, 1936, vol. 4, 236 in *Non-violence in Peace and War*, vol. 1 (1949), 127–128.

8. Bhikhu Parekh, *Gandhi's Political Philosophy* (London: Macmillan, 1989), 57.

9. Ibid., 58.

10. Rabindranath Tagore, *Home and the World* (New Delhi: Macmillan India, 1919, repr., 1983), 22.

11. Ibid., 25–26.

12. M. K. Gandhi, in *Harijan*, November 11, 1947, in *Non-violence in Peace and War*, vol. 2, 1949, 336.

13. M. K. Gandhi, *An Autobiography: The Story of My Experiments with Truth* (Boston: Beacon Hill, 1957), 265.

14. M. K. Gandhi, *CWMG*, 22: 412–413.

15. M. K. Gandhi, *All Men are Brothers*, Krishna Kriplani, ed. (New York: Continuum, 1990), 81.

16. M. K. Gandhi, *An Autobiography*, 4.

17. *Young India* (October 27, 1927).

18. Dinanath G. Tendulkar, *Mahatma: Life of Mohandas Karamchand Gandhi*, vol. 8, (Publications Division of the Ministry of Information, 1951–1954), 331–332.

19. *Harijan* (April 29, 1939).

20. Ramchandra K. Prabhu & U. R. Rao, (eds.), *The Mind of Mahatma Gandhi* (Ahmedabad: Navajivan Publishing 1967), 39.

21. Jawaharlal Nehru, *Nehru on Gandhi*, op. cit., 61.

22. N. K. Bose, *Selections from Gandhi* (Ahmedabad: Navajivan Publishing House, 1968), 37.

23. See M. K. Gandhi, *Trusteeship* (Ahmedabad: Navajivan Publishing House, 1960).

24. Ibid., 22.

25. *Harijan* (February 1, 1942).

26. Quoted by Kuruvilla Pandikattu, "Sevagramand Sarvodaya: Gandhian Symbols for Future" in Kuruvilla Pandikattu, *Gandhi: The Meaning of Mahatma for the Millennium* (Washington: The Council for Research in Values and Philosophy, 2001), 203–204.

27. Shriman Narayan, ed., *The Selected Works of Mahatma Gandhi*, vol. 6 (Ahmedabad: Navajivan Publishing House, 1968), 386.

28. *Harijan* (September 9, 1939).

29. M. K. Gandhi, *Documents on Social, Moral and Spiritual Values in Education*, (New Delhi: NCERT, 1979), 20.

30. *Young India* (July 30, 1931), 199.

31. Raghavan N. Iyer, ed., *The Essential Writings of Mahatma Gandhi* (Delhi: Oxford University Press, 1993), 109.

FIVE   *Gandhi's Reception in India*

1. See Rajmohan Gandhi, *Mohandas: A True Story Of The Man, His People And An Empire* (Delhi: Penguin, 2006), 622.

2. Quoted in T. V. Parvate, "Bhirmrao Ranji Ambedkar" in *Political Thinkers of Modern India*, vol. 16, Verinder Grover, ed. (New Delhi: Deep & Deep Publications, 1992), 249–250.

3. *Young India*, December 8, 1920, in *CWMG*, 19 (Navajivan, Ahmedabad: 1966), 83–85.

4. Christophe Jaffrelot, *Dr. Ambedkar and Untouchability: Analysing and Fighting Caste* (Delhi: Permanent Black, 2004), 63.

5. Quoted in Vasant Moon (ed.), *Dr. Babasaheb Ambedkar: Writings and Speeches*, Dept. of Education, Government of Maharashtra, vol. 2 (Bombay, 1982), 663.

6. Ibid., 94.

7. Quoted in R. Guha, *An Anthropologist Among the Marxists and Other Essays* (Delhi: Permanent Black, 2002), 98.

8. B. R. Ambedkar, *What Congress and Gandhi Have Done to the Untouchables* (Bombay: Thacker & Co, 1945), 284, 289.

9. Quoted in Sangharakshita Mahathera, "Dr. Babasaheb Ambedkar and Buddhism," in *Political Thinkers of Modern India*, 216.

10. Quoted in D. Keer, *Dr. Ambedkar: Life and Mission* (2nd ed.) (Bombay: Popular Prakashan, 1962), 166.

11. M. K. Gandhi, *CWMG*, 84: 272, quoted in Rajmohan Gandhi, *Mohandas: A True Story* , (New Delhi: Publications Division), 525.

12. Rajmohan Gandhi, *Mohandas: A True Story* , 411.

13. Quoted in Gail Minault, *The Khilafat Movement: Religious Symbolism and Political Mobilization in India* (Delhi: OUP, 1982), 68.

14. Quoted in M. H. Sayid, *Mohammad Ali Jinnah*, Shaikh Muhammad Ashraf (Lahore: 1945), 264–265.

15. Quoted in L. A. Sherwani, ed., *Pakistan Resolution to Pakistan* (Karachi: National Publishing House Limited, 1969), 78.

16. Das Durga, *From Curzon to Nehru and Afterwards* (London: Collins, 1969), 353.

17. M. A. Karandikar, *Islam in India's Transition to Modernity* (New Delhi: Orient Longman, 1968), preface, 7.

18. See A. A. Rauoof, *Meet Mr. Jinnah* (Ashraf, Lahore: 1944), 3.

19. See Surendra Bhana, Vahed, and Goolman, *The Making of a Political Reformer: Gandhi in South Africa 1893–1914* (Manohar, New Delhi: 2005), 143.

20. D. G. Tendulkar, *Abdul Ghaffar Khan Faith is a Battle* (Bombay: Gandhi Peace Foundation, 1967), 291.

21. Talk delivered by Hans Küng on March 31, 2005, at the opening of the Exhibit on the World's Religions at Santa Clara University, http://www.scu.edu/ethics/practicing/focusareas/global_ethics/laughlin-lectures/kung-world-religions.html.

22. M. K. Gandhi, *Harijan* (July 8, 1933).

23. M. K. Gandhi, *An Autobiography* (Navajivan, Ahmedabad: 1927), 615–617.

24. B. G. Tilak, *Selected Documents of Lokamanya Bal Gangadhar Tilak, 1880–1920* (New Delhi: Anmol Publications, vol. 1), 106.

25. Judith M. Brown, *Gandhi: Prisoner of Hope* (New Haven: Yale University Press, 1989), 309.

26. Ian Henderson Douglas, *Abul Kalam Azad: An Intellectual and Religious Biography* (Delhi: Oxford University Press, 1988), 54.

27. Ibid., 78.

28. Quoted in Abdul Waheed Khan: *India Wins Freedom, the Other Side* (Karachi: 1961), 22–23.

29. Maulana Azad, *India Wins Freedom* (Longmans, Green and Co., 1960), 169.

30. Quoted in Rasheedudin Khan, *Portrait of a Great Patriot: Maulana Abul Kalam Azad* (1888–1958) in Verinder Grover, *Political Thinkers of India*, vol. 17 (New Delhi: Deep & Deep Publications, 1992), 208–209.

31. K. M. Yusuf, *Maulana Abul Kalam Azad* in Verinder Grover, *Political Thinkers*, 374.

32. Quoted in Ian Henderson Douglas, *Abul Kalam Azad* (Delhi: Oxford University Press, 1988), 276.

33. Sheila McDonough, *Gandhi's Responses to Islam* (New Delhi: D. K. Printworld, 1994), 77.

34. Quoted in D. G. Tendulkar, *Mahatma: A Life of Mohandas Karamchand Gandhi*, (New Delhi: Government of India, vol. 6, Ministry of Information and Broadcasting, 1962), 155.

35. M. K. Gandhi, *The Hindu-Muslim Unity* (Bombay: Bharatiya Vidya Bhavan, 1965), 66.

36. Ibid., 47–49.

37. Abdul Ghaffar Khan, *My Life and Struggle, Autobiography Abdul Ghaffar Khan* (Delhi: Orient Paperbacks, 1969), 27–28.

38. Ibid., 144–145.

39. D. G. Tendulkar, *Abdul Ghaffar Khan* (Bombay: 1967), 48.

40. Ibid., 93–94.

41. Sayed Wiqar Ali Shah, *Ethnicity, Islam and Nationalism: Muslim Politics in the North-West Frontier Province 1937–1947* (Karachi, Oxford University Press, 1999–2000), 27–28.

42. J. S. Bright, *Frontier and Its Gandhi* (Lahore: 1944), 103–104.

43. Quoted in *CWMG*, 72: 277–278.

44. Ibid., 277–279.

45. Quoted in Margaret Chatterjee, *Gandhi's Religious Thought* (London: The Macmillan Press, 1983), 179.

46. *Harijan* (September 29, 1940).

47. Ibid.

48. Quoted in Anil Nauriya, "Gandhi on Secular Law and State": *The Hindu* (Wednesday, October 22, 2003).

49. Quoted in "The Gandhi Myth," http://library.flawlesslogic.com/gandhi.htm.

50. Jawaharlal Nehru, *Nehru on Gandhi* (New York: The John Day Company, 1948), 83.

SIX   *Gandhi and Beyond*

1. M. K. Gandhi, *Non-violence in Peace and War*, vol. 1 (Ahmedabad: Navajivan Publishing House, 1942), 124.

2. Martin Luther King, "Our Struggle" in *A Testament of Hope: The Essential Writings of Martin Luther King, Jr.* (San Francisco: Harper & Row, 1986), 77.

3. Martin Luther King, *Stride Toward Freedom: The Montgomery Story* (New York: Harper & Row, 1958), 100.

4. Martin Luther King, "Pilgrimage to Nonviolence" in *A Testament of Hope*, 40.

5. Martin Luther King, *Stride Toward Freedom*, 104.

6. Martin Luther King, "Facing the Challenge in a New Age," in *A Testament of Hope*, 140.

7. Martin Luther King, *Stride Toward Freedom*, 97.

8. M. K. Gandhi, Navajivan, December 4, 1921, in *CWMG*, 21: 519–520.

9. M. K. Gandhi, *CWMG*, 48: 411–412.

10. Martin Luther King "The Ethical Demands For Integration," in *A Testament of Hope*, 122.

11. Martin Luther King, "Where Do We Go From Here?" in *A Testament of Hope*, 626.

12. Ibid., 626.

13. M. K. Gandhi, *From Yeravda Mandir* (Ahmedabad: Navajivan Publishing, 1937), 25.

14. Martin Luther King, "Where Do We Go From Here?" in *A Testament of Hope*, 620.

15. Martin Luther King, "The Rising Tide of Racial Consciousness" in *A Testament of Hope*, 151.

16. Martin Luther King, "Suffering and Faith," in *A Testament of Hope*, 41.

17. Martin Luther King, "The American Dream," in *A Testament of Hope*, 218.

18. Ibid., 217–218.

19. M. K. Gandhi, *Harijan* (March 23, 1940).

20. Martin Luther King, *Strength to Love* (New York: Harper & Row Publishers, 1958), 64.

21. Martin Luther King, "Honoring Dr. Du Bois," in *Freedomways*, vol. 8 (spring 1968), 110–111.

22. Greg Moses, *Revolution of Conscience: Martin Luther King, Jr. and the Philosophy of Nonviolence* (New York: The Guildford Press, 1997), 202.

23. Nelson Mandela, *Long Walk to Freedom: The Autobiography of Nelson Mandela* (London: Little, Brown and Company, 1994), 147.

24. Nelson Mandela, "The Sacred Warrior," *Time*, December 31, 1999, 96, quoted in David Hardiman, *Gandhi in His Time and Ours: The Global Legacy of His Ideas* (London: Hurst & Company, 2003), 279.

25. Nelson Mandela, *Long Walk to Freedom*, 552.

26. See Michael Battle, *Reconciliation: The Ubuntu Theology of Desmond Tutu* (Cleveland, Ohio: Pilgrim Press, 1997), 39.

27. Desmond Tutu, *God Has A Dream: A Vision of Hope for Our Time* (New York: Doubleday), 27.

28. Desmond Tutu, "Jesus Christ Life of the World," Women's Colloquium, June 17, 1982, quoted in J. B. Hill, *The Theology of Martin Luther King, Jr. and Desmond Mpilo Tutu* (New York: Palgrave, 2007), 107.

29. G. Sharp, *The Role of Power in Nonviolent Struggle, Monograph Series, No. 3* (The Albert Einstein Institution, 1990), 18.

SEVEN   *Conclusion*

1. M. K. Gandhi, *All Men Are Brothers* (Ahmedabad: Navajivan Trust, 1960), 187.

2. M. K. Gandhi, *Harijan* (August 11, 1940), 241.

Bibliography

Agarwal, S. N., ed. *Relevance of Gandian Economics*. Ahmedabad: Navajivan Publishing House, 1970.

———. *Sarvodaya: Its Principles and Program*. Ahmedabad: Navajivan Publishing House, 1951.

Ambedkar, B. R. *What Congress and Gandhi Have Done to the Untouchables*. Bombay: Thacker & Co, 1945.

Andrews, C. F. *Mahatma Gandhi: His Own Story*. London: Allen & Unwin, 1930.

———. *Mahatma Gandhi's Ideas*. London: Allen & Unwin, 1929.

Anjarai, J. J. *An Essay on Gandhian Economics*. Bombay: Vora & Co., 1945.

Arendt, H. *Between Past and Future*. New York: Meridian Books, 1965.

Ashe, Geoffrey. *Gandhi: A Study in Revolution*. Bombay: Asia Publishing House, 1968.

Azad, Maulana. *India Wins Freedom:* Longmans, Green and Co., 1960.

Bakshi. S. R. *Gandhi and the Mass Movements*. New Delhi: Atlantic Publishers, 1988.

Bandyopadhyaya, J. *Gandhi: Theory and Practice: Social Impact and Contemporary Relevance*. Shimla: Indian Institute of Advanced Study, 1969.

Basu, S. K. *Foundations of the Political Philosophy of Sarvodaya*. Delhi: Bliss and Light Publishers, 1984.

Battle, Michael. *Reconciliation: The Ubuntu Theology of Desmond Tutu*. Cleveland, Ohio: Pilgrim Press, 1997.

Bhana, Surendra, and Vahed and Goolman. *The Making of a Political Reformer: Gandhi in South Africa 1893–1914*. Manohar: New Delhi, 2005.

Bharathi, K. S. *The Social Philosophy of Mahatma Gandhi*. New Delhi: Concept Publishing Company, 1991.

Bhattacharya, Buddhadeva. *The Evolution of the Political Philosophy of Mahatma Gandhi*. Calcutta: Calcutta Book House, 1969.

Bondurant, Joan. *Conquest of Violence: The Gandhian Philosophy of Conflict*. Rev. ed. Berkeley: University of California Press, 1971.

Borman, William. *Gandhi and Non-Violence*. New York: State University of New York Press, 1986.

Bose, N. K. *Selections from Gandhi*. Ahmedabad: Navajivan Publishing House, 1968.

Bright, J. S. *Frontier and Its Gandhi*. Lahore: 1944.

Brown, Judith M. *Gandhi: Prisoner of Hope*. Yale: 1989.

———. *Gandhi and Civil Disobedience*. London: Cambridge University Press, 1977.

———. *Gandhi's Rise to Power*. Cambridge: University Press, 1972.

Chakravartty, Gargi. *Gandhi: A Challenge to Communalism: A Study of Gandhi and Hindu-Muslim Problem*. New Delhi: Eastern Books, 1991.

Chatterjee, Margaret. *Gandhi's Religious Thought*. University of Notre Dame Press, 1983.

Choudhuri, Manmohan. *Exploring Gandhi*. New Delhi: The Gandhi Peace Foundation, 1989.

Clement, Catherine. *Gandhi: Father of a Nation*. London: Thames & Hudson, 1996.

Dalton, Dennis. *Mahatma Gandhi: Nonviolent Power in Action*. New York: Columbia University Press, 1993.

Das, Durga. *From Curzon to Nehru and Afterwards*. Collins: London, 1969.

Datta, Dhirendra. *The Philosophy of Mahatma Gandhi*. Madison: University of Wisconsin Press, 1961.

Datye, S. N. *Rethinking Mahatma Gandhi: Relevance of Gandhian Thought and Leadership in the 21st Century*. Kalinga Publications: Delhi, 2001.

Devanesan, Chandran. *The Making of the Mahatma*. Bombay: Orient Longmans, 1969.

Dhavan, Gopinath. *The Political Philosophy of Mahatma Gandhi*. Bombay: 1946; reprint, Delhi, 1990.

Diwakar, R. R. *Gandhi is Spirituality in Action*. New Delhi: Gandhi Peace Foundation, 1985.

Douglas, Ian Henderson. *Abul Kalam Azad: An Intellectual and Religious Biography*. Delhi: Oxford University Press, 1988.

Echols, James, ed. *I Have a Dream: Martin Luther King Jr. and the Future of Multicultural America*. Minneapolis: Fortress Press, 2004.

Erikson, Erik H. *Gandhi's Truth: On the Origins of Militant Nonviolence*. New York: W. W. Norton, 1969.

Fischer, Louis. *The Life of Mahatma Gandhi*. New York: 1950.

Gandhi, M. K. *All Men are Brothers*. Kripalani, Krishna, ed. Paris: UNESCO, 1969.

———. *An Autobiography*. Navajivan, Ahmedabad: 1927.

———. *The Collected Works of Mahatma Gandhi* [CWMG]. Publications Division, Ministry of Information, Government of India, 1961.

———. *Documents on Social, Moral and Spiritual Values in Education*. New Delhi: NCERT, 1979.

———. *Ethical Religion*. Madras: S. Ganesan, 1922.

———. *From Yeravda Mandir*. Ahmedabad: Navajivan Publishing, 1937.

———. *Hind Swaraj and Other Writings*. Anthony J. Parel, ed. Cambridge: Cambridge University Press, 1997.

———. *The Hindu-Muslim Unity*. Bombay: Bharatiya Vidya Bhavan, 1965.

———. *Non-Violence in Peace and War*, vol. 2. ed. Ahmedabad: Bharatan Kumarappa, 1942.

———. *Satyagraha in South Africa*. Ahmedabad, Navajivan: 1928.

———. *Selected Political Writings*. Dennis Dalton, ed. Indianapolis: Hackett Publishing Company, 1996.

———. *Towards Everlasting Peace*. A. T. Hingorani, ed. Bombay: Bharatiya Vidya Bhavan, 1956.

———. *Trusteeship*. Ahmedabad: Navjivan Publishing House, 1960.

Gandhi, Rajmohan. *The Good Boatman*. New Delhi: Penguin Books, 1997.

———. *Mohandas: A True Story of a Man, His People and an Empire*. New Delhi: Penguin Books, 2006.

———. *Understanding the Muslim World*. New Delhi: Penguin Books, 1987.

Ganguli, B. N. *Gandhi's Social Philosophy: Perspective and Relevance*. New Delhi: Council for Social Development, 1973.

Guha, R. *An Anthropologist Among the Marxists and other Essays*. Delhi: Permanent Black, 2002.

Hardiman, David. *Gandhi in His Time and Ours: The Global Legacy of His Ideas*. London: Hurst & Company, 2003.

Hill, J. B. *The Theology of Martin Luther King, Jr. and Desmond Mpilo Tutu*. New York: Palgrave, 2007.

Hingorani, Anand T., ed. *The Supreme Power*. Bombay: Pearl Publications, 1963.

Iyer, Raghavan. *The Moral and Political Thought of Mahatma Gandhi*. New York: Oxford University Press, 1973.

Jaffrelot, Christophe. *Dr. Ambedkar and Untouchability: Analysing and Fighting Caste*. Delhi: Permanent Black, 2004.

Johnson, Richard L. *Gandhi's Experiments with Truth*. Oxford: Lexington Books, 2006.

Karandikar, M. A. *Islam in India's Transition to Modernity*. New Delhi: Orient Longman, 1968.

Keer, Dhananjay. *Dr. Ambedkar: Life and Mission*. 2nd ed. Bombay: Popular Prakashan, 1962.

———. *Mahatma Gandhi: Political Saint and Unarmed Prophet*. Bombay: 1973.

Khan, Abdul Ghaffar. *My Life and Struggle, Autobiography of Abdul Gaffar Khan*. Delhi: Orient Paperbacks, 1969.

Khan, Abdul Waheed. *India Wins Freedom, the Other Side*. Karachi: 1961.

King, Martin Luther. "Our Struggle" in *A Testament of Hope: The Essential Writings of Martin Luther King, Jr.* San Francisco: Harper & Row, 1986.

———. *Strength to Love*. New York: Harper & Row, 1958.

———. *Stride Toward Freedom: The Montgomery Story*. New York: Harper & Row, 1958.

Kripalani, Krishna. *Gandhi: A Life*. 1968; reprint. New Delhi: National Book Trust, 1982.

Mandela, Nelson. *Long Walk to Freedom: The Autobiography of Nelson Mandela*. London: Little, Brown and Company, 1994.

Mathai, M. P. *Mahatma Gandhi's World-View*. New Delhi: Gandhi Peace Foundation, 2000.

McDonough, Sheila. *Gandhi's Responses to Islam*. New Delhi: D. K. Printworld, 1994.

Merton, Thomas, ed. *Gandhi on Non-Violence*. New York: New Directions, 1965.

Minault, Gail. *The Khilafat Movement: Religious Symbolism and Political Mobilization in India*. Delhi: OUP, 1982.

Moon, Vasant, ed. *Dr. Babasaheb Ambedkar: Writings and Speeches*, vol. 2. Bombay: Dept. of Education, Government of Maharashtra, 1982.

Moses, Greg. *Revolution of Conscience: Martin Luther King, Jr. and the Philosophy of Nonviolence*. New York: The Guildford Press, 1997.

Murthy, Srinivas. *Mahatma Gandhi and Leo Tolstoy Letters*. Long Beach: Long Beach Publications, 1987.

Nanda, B. R. *Gandhi and His Critics*. New Delhi: Oxford University Press, 1985.

———. *In Search of Gandhi*. New Delhi: Oxford University Press, 2002.

———. *Mahatma Gandhi: A Biography*. 1st ed., 1958; exp. ed. New Delhi: Oxford University Press, 1981.

Narayan, Shrinam, ed. *Selected Works of Mahatma Gandhi*, vol. 71. Ahmedabad: Navijavan Publishing House, 1969.

Nehru, Jawaharlal. *Nehru on Gandhi*. New York: The John Day Company, 1948.

Noorani, A. G. *Savarkar and Hindutva*. New Delhi: Left Word, 2002.

Pandikattu, K. *Gandhi: The Meaning of Mahatma for the Millennium*. Washington: The Council for Research in Values and Philosophy, 2001.

Parekh, Bhikhu. *Colonialism, Tradition and Reform: An Analysis of Gandhi's Political Discourse*. New Delhi: Sage, 1989.

———. *Gandhi*. New Delhi: Oxford University Press, 1997.

———. *Gandhi's Political Philosophy: A Critical Examination*. London: Macmillan, 1989; reprint, Columbus, Missouri: South Asia Books, 1996.

Prabhu, Ramchandra K. & Rao, U. R., eds. *The Mind of Mahatma Gandhi*. Ahmedabad: Navajivan Publishing, 1967.

Rauoof, A. A. *Meet Mr. Jinnah*. Ashraf, Lahore: 1944.

Roy, Ramashray. *Self and Society: A Study in Gandhian Thought*. New Delhi; Beverly Hills: Sage Publications in collaboration with United Nations University, Tokyo, 1984, c1985.

Sayid, M. H. *Mohammad Ali Jinnah*. Shaikh Muhammad Ashraf, Lahore: 1945.

Shah, Sayed Wiqar Ali. *Ethnicity, Islam and Nationalism: Muslim Politics in the North-West Frontier Province 1937–1947*. Karachi, Oxford University Press, 1999–2000.

Sharp, G. *The Role of Power in Nonviolent Struggle, Monograph Series, No. 3*. The Albert Einstein Institution, 1990.

Sherwani, L. A. ed. *Pakistan Resolution to Pakistan*. Karachi: National Publishing House Limited, 1969.

Tagore, Rabindranath. *Home and the World*. New Delhi: Macmillan India, 1919; reprint, 1983.

Tendulkar, D. G. *Abdul Ghaffar Khan Faith is a Battle*. Bombay: Gandhi Peace Foundation, 1967.

———. *Mahatma: Life of Mohandas Karamchand Gandhi*, vol. 7; October 1946. Bombay: Vithalbhai K. Jhaveri, 1953.

Terchek, Ronald J. *Gandhi: Struggling for Autonomy*. Lanham, Maryland: Rowman & Littlefield, 1999.

Tilak, B. G. *Selected Documents of Lokamanya Bal Gangadhar Tilak, 1880–1920*. New Delhi: Anmol Publications.

Tutu, Desmond. *God Has A Dream: A Vision of Hope for Our Time.*
New York: Doubleday, 2004.

Verinder, Grover, ed. *Political Thinkers of Modern India*, vol. 16. New
Delhi: Deep & Deep Publications, 1992.

Weil, Eric. *Logique de la Philosophie.* Vrin: 1967.

....

Acknowledgments

With any book, the debts of an author are numerous and largely unpaid. There has been a flourish of literary works on Gandhi over the past fifty years that has made finding any new and original approach to his thought and action a true scholarly challenge. I began to address this challenge more than ten years ago with my first book on Gandhi, written in French, and entitled *Gandhi: Aux sources de la nonviolence* (Paris: Felin, 1999), a volume that explicitly addressed the issue of Western intellectual influences on Gandhi. For the past twenty years of my life as a scholar, a writer, and a civil-society activist, I have been struggling with different angles of Gandhian nonviolence both academically and politically. My personal and philosophical proximity with Indian society and civilization helped lay the intellectual foundations for this book. My colleagues and friends at the Centre for the Study of Developing Societies in

Delhi offered a vibrant community in which I had a chance to try out new ideas and explore new dimensions of Gandhian thought. My dearest friend and colleague, Ashis Nandy, provided consistent guidance and encouragement. I was also fortunate to benefit from the thoughtful comments and stimulating suggestions of my Indian friends Sudhir Kakar, Raj Rewal, and Rajmohan Gandhi. They opened my eyes to another view of Gandhi and India.

The various chapters that comprise this book also reflect a series of reflections arising from exchanges and debates with scholars and friends, including Fred Dallmayr, Michael Ignatieff, Giancarlo Bosetti, Guiliano Amato, Emma Bobino, Tzvetan Todorov, and Shlomo Avineri.

As so often before, I want to thank the University of Toronto, and especially The Centre for Ethics and its supportive director, Melissa Williams. Melissa has herself been brilliantly exploring many of the issues that underpin the inquiry of this book.

I am also indebted to the Department of Political Science at University of Toronto and its friendly chair, David Cameron, for financial support and intellectual input.

I also want to thank a series of editorial contributions by Richie Nojang Khatami, who did his best to clarify my prose and who took charge of the manuscript in its different stages in an impressively efficient manner.

My sincere thanks to Ian Malcolm, my friend and editor at Harvard University Press, without whose help this book would not have been possible. This book would not be what it is today without his support and advice.

Finally, I am profoundly grateful to my family. My wife, Azin Moalej, has been a most loving companion and partner in all that I have done in recent years. Her love, support, and encouragement are clear signs of her fortitude in putting up with the necessarily idiosyncratic habits of an intellectual. Last but not least, I want to thank my mother, Khojasteh Kia, who bequeathed to me so much, including many of the virtues— honesty, discipline, and determination—essential to scholarship. There are many echoes of her influence in these pages.

By acknowledging so many, I am not trying to share the blame for what remains. The subject matter I have addressed lends itself to many interpretations. Undoubtedly, also, my perspective is expressive of my intercultural background and especially due to my intellectual and political experiences in countries like Iran and India.

Index